The Soul's Intent

Also by Ernie Vecchio

Big Tail, Small Kite: The Wisdom of Balance

The Soul's Intent

✦

An Interview with the Divine

Ernie Vecchio,
Licensed Counseling Psychologist

iUniverse, Inc.
New York Bloomington Shanghai

The Soul's Intent
An Interview with the Divine

Copyright © 2008 by Ernie Vecchio

All rights reserved. No part of this book may be used or reproduced by any means, graphic, electronic, or mechanical, including photocopying, recording, taping or by any information storage retrieval system without the written permission of the publisher except in the case of brief quotations embodied in critical articles and reviews.

iUniverse books may be ordered through booksellers or by contacting:

iUniverse
1663 Liberty Drive
Bloomington, IN 47403
www.iuniverse.com
1-800-Authors (1-800-288-4677)

Because of the dynamic nature of the Internet, any Web addresses or links contained in this book may have changed since publication and may no longer be valid.

The views expressed in this work are solely those of the author and do not necessarily reflect the views of the publisher, and the publisher hereby disclaims any responsibility for them.

ISBN: 978-0-595-50012-3 (pbk)
ISBN: 978-0-595-49605-1 (cloth)
ISBN: 978-0-595-61341-0 (ebk)

Printed in the United States of America

In a class all of its own. A book that encourages that we cannot be present until we choose to get here. A spiritual message for everyone.
—Don Swick

A guiding discussion through the maze of absence to the joy of presence

Recognize divine intent. Learn contradictory truths. Learn what drives and fuels your passion. Access your inner life—and much more ...

As far as we can discern, the sole purpose of human existence is to kindle a light in the darkness of mere being.
—C. G. Jung
Memories, Dreams, Reflections

Contents

Acknowledgments ix
Introduction xi

CHAPTER 1 The Wound 3
  Developing insight from your life experiences 3

CHAPTER 2 Illusions and Inner Dialogue 9
  Realizing that distractions prevent a context that is true 9

CHAPTER 3 Ego Motivations 19
  Supporting your weaker or less-expressed abilities 19

CHAPTER 4 Shadow 23
  Coming out of the darkness 23

CHAPTER 5 (E)motions 33
  Building a bridge between the spiritual and the emotional 33

CHAPTER 6 Mastering Fear 41
  Part One Improvising to seek comfort and find presence 41
  Part Two Witnessing and attending to pain so you can grow 44

CHAPTER 7 Inner Images: Witnessing Spiritual Work 49
  Taming, awakening, and guiding you to the present 49

CHAPTER 8 Resistance 57
  Part One Realizing that the opposite of resistance is freedom 57
  Part Two Seeing through the imaginary veil of the ego 59
  Part Three Choosing self-love over the ego's distractions 61

CHAPTER 9 Letting Go of Expectations 65

    Hearing the ego turn up the volume; feeling the soul turn up the heat. 65

Chapter 10   Activating Divinity. 69
    Gaining confidence that we can feel and be better 69

Chapter 11   Forgiveness and Mercy. 75
    Part One Placing ourselves in good standing with our personal truth. 75
    Part Two Combining leniency with compassion for mercy to the self 76
    Part Three Empowering ourselves to make better decisions 77

Chapter 12   Truth and Hidden Influences. 81
    Understanding that we need not know how to be because there is a model for
        wholeness in the soul's memory 81

Chapter 13   Patience. 89
    Accepting that anything less than patience fuels self-loathing. 89

Chapter 14   Things Happen for a Reason 97
    Part One Aligning our inner and outer worlds with meaningful coincidence 97
    Part Two Realizing that true nature is recovered through vulnerability 99

Chapter 15   Presence. 103
    Part One Observing the play of thoughts, feelings, hopes, and fears. 103
    Part Two Intuitively healing and restoring the soul to its original state 105

Chapter 16   Movement and Rebirth 109
    Part One Reviving learning, culture conversion, and spiritual awakening. 109
    Part Two Taking the steps to personal and spiritual growth. 111

Chapter 17   The Soul's Intent 117
    Trusting that a visible inner light observes our emotional reactions without
        judgment 117

Epilogue 121

Glossary. 125

Bibliography 129

Acknowledgments

Every book originates and is produced through the efforts of people beyond the author. In my case, they are every person who sought my guidance and shared a journey. It was the richness of their spiritual healing that affirmed this book. My colleague, mentor, and friend Don Swick, with whom I shared many conversations on the topic, helped me clarify my thoughts and feelings. Countless friends and acquaintances, too numerous to mention, have provided insights. To all of these, I offer my thanks and gratitude for their support.

Introduction

Physics describes a candle as a unit of brilliance that has a standard composition equal to 1.02 candelas of light. This visible light reveals itself in the human condition as a divine spark of soul and spirit.

Nerve impulses pass from an axon of one neuron to the dendrite of another. A single beat of the heart pumps blood through our veins. Being alive means to inhale and exhale through our lungs. All of this happens automatically, yet we are not wearing a battery pack. Nor is there an extension cord dangling from our backs. These visible miracles of life are physical expressions of divine energy. Experienced as the human spirit, this energy receives its directions from the soul.

A candle, once lit, or a human once born, needs oxygen to continue. Cut off from this element, the candle or life goes out or dies. Everyone comes into the world as vulnerable as a candle. Existing in a closed container or physical body is its infant beginning. As time passes, the external environment threatens this candle from all sides. Like rings that represent the age of a tree, we create layers of defenses between this candle and the outside world. Each layer represents ego or personality, and, the more defended we become, the less oxygen gets to our candle.

As our sense of self develops we are faced with a conflicting truth: though psychological and emotional warmth may not be available, we are to behave as if it is. The colder our experience, the more we can only imagine the warmth of love. Naïve as children about such matters, we slowly develop feelings of inadequacy and unworthiness. Poor teachers and emotional neglect leave us cold before our feet can barely touch the ground. This fearful and vulnerable place marks the beginning of a spiritual journey for many people.

The Soul's Intent teaches that spiritual maturity is a personal struggle toward presence—toward living in the *now*. The conflicting qualities include an obliviously childish entity (the ego) that drives us, spiritual energy that motivates our actions (emotions), and a soul that orchestrates the journey.

The soul knows we live in a three-dimensional reality with a brain that interacts with the world two-dimensionally. It scripts in characters and experiences for us to see what we need to see. In this larger perspective, we can walk between the worlds of matter and spirit. From the soul's vantage point, a spiritual crisis exists when the ego is in charge of our journey. Typically, this means that we are obsessing in our heads and away from our bodies. Unaware of this absence, we identify with our thoughts and miss the most important part of who we are. Eventually, we carry the guilt of our own separation. To offset these internal feelings of division, the soul wants us to see what is happening. This means understanding how the ego is using the background (past) to see the foreground (present) of our lives. Awareness is witnessing both simultaneously. While the ego gives ultimatums, the soul offers compromise as an alternative. Its wish is that we put less emphasis on ego patterns and cultivate the basic human ethic of compassion.

Throughout this book we will witness a conversation between the ego (the seeker) and soul (the divine). The *ego* is defined as an aspect of the self that seeks balance in its known reality. Unable to see its own reflection, it can only become self-aware when communicating with its above observer or divine essence—the *soul*. Figuratively higher than or superior to the ego, the soul observes our lives without judgment or analysis. The ego's inability to recognize itself or to see what it is doing makes it a seeker. Sensitive to the memories and emotions of its experiences, the ego questions everything a person thinks, feels, or does. Because the soul or diving encompasses all that can be intuitively perceived, it organizes our dream symbols into a series of answers. The context these symbols provide allows for a deeper understanding of our lives. Thus, it is the soul that provides us support when the ego doubts its choices. Without a connection to this larger perspective, many of us stay trapped in the past. The personality tends to seek a higher source when it is suffering. The soul's intent is that we understand our journey when things are going well.

The spiritual implication of the ideas presented in this book is no accident. Understanding personal struggles through symbols offers a living motion picture of a seeker's inner life. It offers hope that we need not punish ourselves for not living life a certain way. The soul knows that life is the most meaningful when we can see the *whole* of our experiences. It is this perspective that brings oxygen to our candle. Accessing this inner spark isn't about redemption; it is more about taking hold of one's true nature.

The Soul's Intent uses dream content as a prescriptive map to self-discovery and healing. All contributors were seekers working their way into the present. Be mindful that the same intelligence that instructed your cells at conception arranged these dream symbols into answers of spiritual guidance. The implication is that such symbols emanate from a divine source within the unconscious. C. G. Jung was the founder of the school of analytical psychology. He states, "… I realize that the unconscious is a process, and that the psyche [soul] is transformed …

by the relationship of the ego to the contents of the unconscious ... that transformation can be read from dreams ... In collective life it has left its deposit principally in the various religious systems and their changing symbols." Jung goes on to say, "Our psyche [soul] is set up in accord with the structure of the universe, and what happens in the macrocosm likewise happens in the infinitesimal and most subjective reaches of the psyche." It is my hope that these subjective inner experiences speak to you and provide meaning to a life that is larger than you imagined.

Ernie Vecchio is a licensed clinical, school, and rehabilitation psychologist with over thirty years experience in the helping profession. He currently lives in Charleston, West Virginia, where he teaches others the worth of knowing their inner selves through a process called Innerscape. Vecchio developed this process of "depth-work" while treating severe trauma patients and leading them to a spiritual understanding of their inner life.

Intention #1

Let go of painful ego perceptions.

1

The Wound

Developing insight from your life experiences

Throughout my career I have examined the "source wound" or first trauma that cuts us away from the creator and our divine uniqueness. For many, understanding the origin and nature of these wounds begins a process of spiritual awakening. Most feel their first wound offers a benchmark to begin their healing.

I once conducted a workshop during which I was asked by a hundred people: "How did you resolve these earlier experiences in yourself?"

My own response is this: "In truth, my life has been nothing more than a mirror image of many people's lives. Yes, I had a dysfunctional beginning with all the related abuses. But, my emotional pain was no different from that of everybody else I have met—personally or professionally. Background or economic advantage did not matter. In essence, spiritual people know what they are. Who they are is another question."

To teach this point, I asked the participants to close their eyes and image the instrument used to cut an umbilical cord at birth. Keeping their eyes closed, several people raised their hands to respond. One responded, "I see a scalpel." Another said, "How about a sharp pair of scissors?" As this is the usual instrument and expected response, I then directed the audience to change the image. During their imagining, I suggested, "Now, I want you to image a hacksaw or a chainsaw." Many of the participants began to squirm in their seats, especially the women. I suggested further: "Now, change the image to a toothbrush or a hatchet." As these images settled into their minds, I asked them to verbalize what they were feeling. The responses were typically "It's bloody and gross!" or "It is more painful and lingering." In this moment I offered my answer, "In the beginning, it seems everyone experiences a cutting away from the creator. The only distinction that sets us apart as people is the instrument used in the cutting." I explained further: "For some, it is quick and clean. For others, it is painful and lasts longer." No matter the instrument used, spiritual seekers spend their lives trying to heal the disconnection.

As the ego seeks spiritual balance in its separation from the source, the soul can provide answers. To help you understand how this can happen, I have presented in each chapter a conversation between the seeker (the ego) and the divine (our own divinity, the soul). The ego can become self-aware only if it communicates with its above observer—the soul. The soul's guidance is connected to the divine, which encompasses all that can be intuitively perceived, and offers the ego a larger context of existence. Without the soul, the ego is trapped in the past. The sequence of the conversation reflects a logical path of spiritual revelation and rebirth. *The Soul's Intent* demonstrates that a wonderful higher organizing intelligence is at work in our lives.
The conversation begins ...

Seeker: Why do we feel emptiness in or around our stomach? Is this the first "source wound"?

Divine: Yes, the area around the stomach is your first source wound. It is unconscious grief associated with loss. First, you lose contact with the creator, and later lose yourself to a forming identity (ego). The two happen close together. Personality (ego) forms between birth and the age of six. It later crystallizes as identity between the ages of nine and twelve. You will spend all your life acting out or discarding these qualities. Though getting cut away is a given for everyone, the identities you show are unique to your personal history. It is this personal history and related suffering that amass with the source wound. The soul pours itself into a container called personality. It starts as clay and later becomes hardened ceramic. The spiritual question: Are you the container or its contents? The soul teaches that you must let go of personality before you can discover your true essence. The soul's image for this growth is a climbing spiral, not a repetitious circle. The ego reenacts life because it has no sense of where it is going. The container must stay intact to avoid certain death of the ego. Examining your source wound, and its exponential growth into the present, brings forgiveness and self-acceptance. As this occurs, you can move away from the patterns of personality. Upward movement occurs when you gain depth from your suffering. Without awareness, there is no beginning and no end to suffering except physical death. This is the problem. Many religious people feel that life will be better after death. Sadly, this implies that life is miserable now.

Seeker: So, this source wound becomes an entry wound that other wounds can affect?

Divine: Yes, but the source wound is unconscious, while the later ones are not. Most people experience them, but they differ in circumstances, degree, and intensity. Importantly, the wound is not *who* you are but simply something that happened to you. Nobody escapes this experience because egos begin as fragile and vulnerable. This explains your hardened container of personality, as it protects you even as you pour into it. Ironically, that which protects eventually imprisons. Just know this: *you* are seeking and understanding its contents! You are not away, just distracted. All human beings, no matter the nature of their beginnings, use their egos for survival. Survival can be an extension of the original wound because the personality, with all of its wants and needs, fears re-injury. Essentially, ego encases your true nature for self-protection. The number of ways in which the ego can trick you away from finding this out is infinite. You can spend a lifetime remembering, learning, then choosing to unlearn what you thought represented your authenticity. The good news: The soul is eternal. Normal laws of time do not apply here. To the soul, you have been absent for only a moment.

Seeker: Does this wound foster self-abuse?

Divine: It can. If you spend years making choices through the lens of the ego, you will not be able to avoid negative effects. Few figure out that the secret is to learn from our choices. They are, more often than not, scripted by the soul for a lesson. The soul wishes for you to internalize your experiences as insight. Instead, most choose to live life by hindsight. Ironically, culture teaches that hindsight is 20-20: perfect vision. Insight and foresight are closer to perfection and truth. The ego conditions you through self-blame and self-punishment—making mistakes fosters guilt, and becoming a mistake fosters shame. This is self-abuse. The outward fear of exposure evolves into an internal experience of abandonment. This takes you farther away from your true nature and spiritual truth. Each such moment feeds your doubts and gives the ego strength. Many imagine, "If people could see me, they would scream and run away."

Seeker: So, if I understand this correctly, we don't have to push to live in the present—we need only to allow? In fact, we are resisting the pull of our nature—out of fear?

Divine: This is true. It is not necessarily that you have to *do* something to arrive. Instead, it is more that you need to *stop doing*. You are fighting your own arrival. Fighting what is driving you (ego) and denying what is pulling (soul) blocks discovery of the spiritual self. The soul knows the human condition comes with an unavoidable wound. In other words, you do not get to choose *if* you will suffer, you only get to choose *how*. Most people fixate on the "why" and never capture the soul's intent. In fact, suffering is the labor of getting here.

Intention #2:

Realize that your internal and external worlds make a whole life.

2

Illusions and Inner Dialogue

Realizing that distractions prevent a context that is true

Experts say that the average individual thinks sixty thousand thoughts a day, most of which are the same thoughts they thought the day before. This leaves little room for new thinking. Since we are not expressing most of these thoughts outwardly, we are drowning in self-talk. As a result, each of us has a false mental representation of the person we believe ourselves to be.

The brain cannot distinguish whether we are having a physical or mental experience, and register both as "real." Inner dialogue essentially becomes a distorted self-analysis without the choice of review. Abnormal self-perceptions cause a misinterpretation of our experience. If an experience is preceded by a strong emotion like fear, the brain can believe that something is present when, in fact, it is not. Illusions and delusions form from information both seen and heard. An adapted interpretation of your outer world becomes an accepted view of reality. If the deceit of your mind's eye produces a false impression, that impression eventually becomes a subjective false memory. As time passes and you recall your experiences, your brain further falsifies, adds, omits, and substitutes details. This fixed illusion and misrepresentation of reality becomes a personality disorder. Psychology reports that eighty-five percent of us have a fixed image of the self.

Mental rehearsal of what we think and believe never stops. If our thoughts and beliefs repeat as self-loathing or shame, our self worth is denigrated. This causes anger that we may not be able to understand. The answer: negative self-talk combined with the "buzz" of our culture makes it increasingly difficult to distinguish real from imagined fear. The result is that millions of people live with a constant low level of agitation and paranoia.

Being able to distinguish between our inner and outer fears is a measure of our coping skills. When anger and false imagination are in full force, most of us project it onto others. The responsibility for who is doing what to whom gets confusing. Self-talk fuels these projections and influences our words, actions, and ambitions. The goal in spiritual work is to speak and interact with the world from the heart. Since there is a high likelihood that our self-talk is not entirely untrue, we must be keenly aware of these inner private conversations. The heart's perspective ensures that what we are saying internally is honest or truthful. It is in the heart that truth starts and ends.

Our inner voice can be a constant whisper or a steady scream. Understanding and controlling this voice is vital in preserving mental health. Ego and the illusions the ego manufactures contribute to a complex process of self-justification. Human beings are thinking animals. Filtered by the ego, the human's goal is to distract itself away from our inner selves and to avoid presence—living in the *now*.

Seeker: I feel that my ego blinds me at times. Is this accurate?

Divine: Yes, it is. The ego is a veil or a filter that you look through at your life. The soul knows that this veil skews your view and alters the truth. As you become more aware of your own divinity—as you learn to listen to your soul—such veils come down. You find the view is incredible. You realize that your past, which was in ill repair, has contaminated your present. Once you realize that the present is beautiful, you want to see again.

Seeker: How does this happen?

Divine: You realize that where you are from is not who you are. Your beginnings hold you hostage, make you feel vulnerable to exposure, and prevent self-expression.

Seeker: Are we trapped in our own heads with an image of the person we think we are?

Divine: Something like that. The image is an echo in your head, an echo from the past. In fact, when the echo is gone, you can hear your own breathing. Imagine the number of people who do not even have the presence of mind to hear their own breath?

Seeker: What is this echo from the past?

Divine: The sound of your own voice, ridiculing and judging, is your echo from the past. There is nowhere to hide from this voice. Most say the harder they try not to listen, the louder it becomes, especially if they feel overwhelmed and can't breathe. The echo can become so loud that you can't even hear yourself scream.

Seeker: This sounds horrible. The ego can do this to us?

Divine: Oh, yes, but only in extreme cases. It is hard to escape from yourself. This is one reason many people take medication—to silence their inner voice. This need is the source of many addictions and character flaws. The ego wears many of us down.

Seeker: Why do you think we run from—rather than discover—our personal truths?

Divine: You fear the result of discovering your personal truth. You often say: "What if I don't like *who* I am?" It seems that forgiving others is easier than forgiving yourself.

Seeker: Why do we fight with this so much? We want so much to feel nurtured and loved. Is it because we fear letting people in?

Divine: It is more accurate to say that you fear presence—being in your body and out of your head. This is because self-deception is harder when you are in your body. You want to find love, but cannot love yourself. You want acceptance, but are unable to accept yourself. The louder your inner critic, the more intense this nagging echo of indifference. Sadly, you feel separated and alienated from the best part of the person you are.

Seeker: Do negative emotions play a part in this inner noise?

Divine: Your emotions are not negative or positive—only thoughts are. Emotions send an electrical and biochemical charge to your brain. These charges help repetitive thoughts to become beliefs. Experienced in the external, they feel like the truth. Giving energy to such mental activity is your inner noise. The volume can eat away at you. Emotions and faulty beliefs fuel an ocean of feelings that bubble out of your awareness. The feelings lay in the depths of your unconscious until they are excited. Unknowingly you fear your emotions when, in reality, you become consumed by contaminated thinking.

Seeker: Can you give an example of how our inner self-talk sounds?

Divine: Imagine life reaching out and getting your attention with an unexpected event or misfortune. Awakened in that moment, your emotions (spirit) will speak: "Guilt and shame prevent you from expressing or experiencing the truth of this moment." Your emotions charge the personality (ego) to respond: "I know. I haven't even done anything wrong! This is not my fault." Emotion activates the ego to defend itself. The ego whispers: "If I allow myself to change what I think and feel, I will die! I need to keep my beliefs in place. What I believe may feel restrictive and prison-like, but at least it's familiar." The emotional reaction is always the same: "This is painful. How do I stop the pain?"

Observing the relationship between the ego (personality) and your emotions (spirit) the soul knows that you repeatedly suffer from self-judgment. As a result, you are constantly on trial. The ego is a child who is emotionally defending itself from the past, while your true nature wants to disassociate itself and enter the present. But, the ego's voice is loud: "I am fearful for my self-image. What if I look stupid! I must need to try harder. What I'm doing doesn't seem enough!" The soul views the context of your life as a whole. If you are aware of its guidance, it teaches, "These voices are the inner messages of your father and mother. This was their life sentence, not yours. There is an alternative in the present. Live here—now—and be free."

Seeker: It is a no-brainer who we should be listening to in that conversation! Is this an example of divine essence or soul seeing the truth?

Divine: Yes. Spiritually, many of you know there is another reality than the one you are living. The ego has trouble seeing this and stays confused. All you have to do to live *in* the truth and embrace what the soul knows—now. In essence, remember the source of your pain, grow from its effect, and let it go.

Seeker: The ego is a powerful force. How far will it go to keep us from being in the present?

Divine: That is a good question. The soul knows that once you experience the present and what that means, you will be able to let go of the past. The soul also knows the ego will not allow that to happen without a fight. Simply put, the ego is relentless.

Seeker: The irony is that the ego slows us down, but also pushes us along. True?

Divine: This truth comes after much introspection and self-realization. Yes, emotionally you feel stuck with the ego. Why? Because the relationship depends on old but specific lies and reactions. At the same time, compassionate self-talk is foreign to the ego. This pushes you to restructure or change your inner beliefs. When you do this, you scatter your energy and emote differently. By relaxing your approach toward the self, you can allow the ego to help you spiritually. Developing this relationship with an aspect of the self that you originally rejected is intoxicating. Sages describe this as an experience of self-love. Feelings and inner language become suitable. Comfortable and genuine authenticity is now a possible and positive force. You can own and take responsibility for the person you are.

Seeker: Why can't we see these internal interactions without the help of a guide? Do we know they are happening or do we just ignore them?

Divine: You feel opposing energy in your body all the time. It fuels your dreams while you are sleeping. Feeling is not the same as seeing. The ego is a strong but tiny portion of the total self. It cannot imagine your vastness. It wants to ignore your inner searching. When you feel the sensation of joy, the ego can experience it but may have no idea how it happened. It will imagine that something you did created the feeling. In actuality, it was likely something you stopped doing. The short answer to your question is that it is impossible to be your own mirror. Because the soul will often "shock" you awake, without a guide the ego would interpret your reaction as a flaw or personification of shame. The soul knows that what you keep unconscious eventually plays out as fate. The only way the ego can see what is going on inside is to reenact it on the outside. In other words, the soul's guidance is getting the ego to create externally what you need to see and learn internally. The soul does this to wake you up.

Seeker: We do fear the discomfort of something new or unknown, don't we?

Divine: Yes. The soul knows you are unhappy with the old and there is no way out except learning from and moving through your suffering. The soul teaches that you get stuck between attitudes and beliefs, which block your forward path. The maze consists of confusing ideas, conflicting urges, opposing opinions, and difficulty in finding your way through irrational emotions. The soul wants you to know that your inner guide will not allow you to go backward. Freedom and self-expression are always ahead.

Seeker: Being unconscious is our curse isn't it?

Divine: Most would agree that "the infinite" is big. The curse may be not realizing that eternity is bigger. To the soul, the unconscious is a two-dimensional perspective in a three-dimensional world. Spirituality and quantum physics speak of the existence of multiple dimensions—fourth, fifth, and so on. Spiritual maturity seeks to "walk between" the worlds of matter and spirit. The first step is letting go of everything the ego holds dear—especially false images and ideas of the person you think you are.

Seeker: The melting away or letting go of old identifications can take a lifetime. Is there a set time for this to happen?

Divine: What is most important is that you are seeking a true reflection of yourself—all the time. Yes, a lifetime of an inner need for freedom does move us along quicker. It seems that our passion for change and growth peaks at midlife. Not everybody realizes what is occurring internally; some people try to "fix" externally the uncomfortable feelings of change they are experiencing internally. They change jobs, partners, and homes with little inner satisfaction. The soul knows you are using distraction to cope. The melting you speak of compels compassion, self-love, forgiveness, and acceptance. Avoiding or denying transition internally can pull you under. Recognizing the soul's intent of presence slows this pull enough to allow you to come aground. The soul teaches that, though your emotions can be overwhelming, you are not alone with this energy. You ask about time? It takes years to form the ego identifications of which we speak, but only days, weeks, and months to remove them.

Seeker: Can old ego identifications and inner dialogue exist in a new place?

Divine: No. There is a death of sorts to ego. This is because the ego finds silence to be deafening. The soul knows that death and rebirth are natural cycles of life. The death of old identifications represents the rebirth of presence. It is a process of self-acceptance. The illusions and inner dialogue of the ego get their energy from guilt and shame. Rejecting and trying not to identify with guilt and shame become your habit and pattern. Internally, love, acceptance, and forgiveness melt the ego, while it is the heat of anger and frustration that feed it. Compassion allows you to find a balance between the two.

Seeker: Does our inner journey change when we stop doing certain behaviors?

Divine: The inner process does not change, but the context of your life does. Yes, a change in perspective can stop self-defeating behaviors. Remember, your external life is symbolic of what is occurring inside. Being aware of how and when your external and internal lives change is a crucial part of spiritual growth.

Seeker: How much of our self-talk comes from our fathers and mothers?

Divine: Parents write the script and direct the drama that is in your head. Most adult children do not want to deal with this, though it is paramount to their healing. The soul knows that if you do not examine these associations and dissolve related ego identities, the drama you inherited will never end. Intimacy issues with the opposite sex may never heal. The soul teaches and reshapes these characters internally. In other words, you, yourself, need to become the father and mother you wished for.

Intention #3:

Recognize the side of your nature that is *capable.*

3

Ego Motivations

Supporting your weaker or less-expressed abilities

Ego is the mistaken notion of "I" as a separate self from which human confusion and suffering come. We experience it as consciousness or identity within the mind. In psychoanalysis, ego is that part of the iceberg visible above the water. Projected as consciousness, we view it as personality. The unconscious is the remaining—and unseen—mass of ice beneath the water. Spiritually, the ego concerns itself with reason, good sense, and rational self-control. If the ego is distorted by family and culture, the result is a personality that is unreasonable, irrational, and lacks common sense.

The ego is the center of "I am" in the human being. It is a complex within the soul that is a person's field of consciousness. Fear based, it is an unnatural aberration of mind that feels it needs to protect personal integrity in an otherwise hostile environment. By design, ego is a psychological disease based on memory and arbitrary assumptions.

The ego's motivations have no single universally accepted definition. In part, the ego concerns itself with intent, effort, and tenacity. It is responsible for the push-pull within the self that is experienced as the battle between the ego (personality) and the soul (nature). Ego motivation is the driving compulsion behind a person's intent. Egos concern themselves with wants, needs, and beliefs that drive their goals. Egos push our mental forces to carry out something, while unsatisfied needs motivate us. At the ego or psychological level, people need understanding, affirmation, support, and appreciation. This positive feedback arouses them to action and gives them purpose and direction in their lives.

Seeker: It seems important to understand the soul's intent and the motivation of the ego—together. Is this true?

Divine: Yes, it is. The soul often presents itself while you are dealing with the rough and smooth aspects of your ego's thoughts and emotions. It teaches you to examine the side of your nature that is capable while you are on the edge of suffering. The soul recognizes ego energy, such as the fear of loss or rejection, as a biochemical charge and uses it for motivation. The ego may experience this as moving against the current (fighting) or avoiding life altogether (flight). The soul knows that living in the present—presence—moves you with the flow rather than against it. It knows you can be fully awake during anxiety. It is important to understand how the soul and ego energies interact.

Seeker: Do you mean that we can be aware of the soul's intent and the ego simultaneously?

Divine: Oh, yes! You have a natural capacity to support yourself while dealing with your weaker or less-frequently-expressed abilities. These negative qualities carry the message that you are not capable. Ego, which was formed in childhood, needs a sympathetic adult perspective today. It is in these moments that the soul can present you with the larger picture. If it does not, your childhood fears consume you.

Seeker: This is the danger of listening only to the ego isn't it?

Divine: Yes. Often, if you review ego thoughts and feelings, they label your life experiences as laden with waste and debris. When this happens, emotions arise. If trust or awareness of your divinity has not developed, you feel alone. Just beneath the surface, the ego can lure you into these emotions. You recall or imagine thoughts of lost potential, and these feed your contempt for the self. You lack the soul's vantage point—its ability to see the whole. There lies the danger.

Seeker: So awareness allows us to trust the inner wisdom of the soul?

Divine: Yes, it is important to know what the soul sees. When you feel free from a painful memory or experience, you have experienced the soul's intent. The ego is insatiable. Its hunger for love, acceptance, and affirmation is constant. Your ego can be insatiable and fixated on the past, and you may not even be aware of this. Awakened to another reality internally, your ego can live in the present.

Intention #4:

Realize that poisons and antidotes are the same.

4

Shadow

Coming out of the darkness

In Jungian psychology, the "shadow" is a quality of the divided individual that results from repressed wishes. It changes after our passion and fire are gone. Essentially, shadow is the memory of lost wants. It is the side of the personality that is largely unseen and unknown. We describe it as "darkness" because it is deeply unconscious. All unconscious layers of the self, both positive and negative, exist within the shadow—especially qualities about ourselves we are not proud of, qualities we deny or disown, or secretly prefer to blame on someone else. Shadow also includes personal characteristics that simply go unrecognized or underdeveloped.

To most of us, a more common understanding of shadow is the painful emotion that results from the awareness of inadequacy or helplessness. This emotional state combines with a set of behaviors that result in intense shame or guilt. We experience humiliation and the loss of self-respect that seem beyond repair. Shadow forms when we are young, and we somehow know it is not our fault. We do not understand how those who love and associate with us can also violate us. The internal corrective feeling for this experience is anger. A human spirit that is not allowed to *be* as the creator intended becomes angry and feels broken. A broken spirit eventually becomes mean-spirited. When we direct this anger inward, we suffer. When we direct this anger outward, everyone suffers.

The relationship between the soul and the shadow is important to understand. The soul is the immaterial part of a person that is the driving cause of an individual life. It is an airy substance particular to a unique living being. Most religions consider the soul immortal but innately aware of its immortal nature. It is our "higher observer" within and outside our body. Shadow is unique to the physical and mortal body, as it needs food, shelter, and water to survive. It is the shadow that struggles with "how much" food, shelter, and water. Our culture teaches the shadow that enough is never enough. Shadow forms when we are young, when anger defends a vulnerable spirit. It represents those qualities of the self that go unrealized. In our waking lives we reject, deny, and project shadow qualities into the world. As a result, it is difficult to see. In our dream-life, however, the shadow visibly interacts with the total self. Its images are important because they allow us to work with and recognize our shadow's contents. According to Carl Jung, the shadow is instinctive and irrational, but not necessarily evil. It can be ruthless in conflict but empathetic in friendship. It is an important quality of our personality, and we benefit by accepting and integrating it into the whole.

In the two-dimensional world of opposites, the balancing principle is the human heart. A compassionate embrace of the dark in ourselves becomes light and love in the world. This is the path to a three-dimensional perspective of life. Love essentially becomes a physical place that we can choose to *be*.

Seeker: It seems that we talk about divine presence following darkness. Why is this?

Divine: Yes, there is a particular mood state that invites divinity. Divine presence is out of view and blocked by the intellectual mind and ego. It is as if you are awake in a dream but asleep in your life. In this way, darkness prevails and keeps you from seeing. The soul brings this into your awareness—if you are paying attention.

Seeker: Is it not true that the emotions of the dark—confusion, frustration, and fear—are where we get our motivation?

Divine: As you mentioned before, the danger lies in listening only to the ego. No one seeks divine guidance in a moment of clarity. The soul knows that you are hiding in the dark. Most forget that their first experience with darkness was in the womb. Your soul knows this. It wants you to remember—the authentic self pulls while your spirit pushes. It is not a coincidence that this is the language of birthing. Getting you here is first contact. Some of us come into the world with a whimper, while others come in with a scream. Even though you are vulnerable and helpless, the soul knows you have great promise—when you awaken to it.

Seeker: We have a sense of this as children, don't we, but can't put it into words? Then, as we get older, we forget. It is almost as if the light of awareness begins to hurt our eyes.

Divine: Whatever happens, most of you decide to shield or protect yourselves from consciousness. The promise of truth and spiritual freedom lies dormant. Most of you sense divine presence in the invisible or close by. But, as quickly as this comes into your awareness, your ego clouds your vision.

Seeker: It is good that the soul doesn't frustrate easily. No one would ever see its intent.

Divine: Yes, this idea about the light coming out of the dark—it's a circle until you are ready to *be* in it. Life assists in this labor of birth everyday.

Seeker: You would think we would want to make life easier. Why do we choose to stay in the dark, even when we know better?

Divine: It seems people need repetition to "get" something. You know that old saying—three times is a charm. People say life happens a particular way for a reason, and never realize why. The shadow is the reason.

Seeker: Once we get it, do we move to the next stage of awareness?

Divine: Yes, but, in an instant, the insight is gone and you fall asleep again. This is how the shadow works. It tries to scare you away from the truth. Sadly, it does this by reminding you what it was like to be little, confused, and helpless. It is in this way that people stay stuck in their past and miss the present. It means the soul has to pull harder.

Seeker: Sounds like we want to go back to the safety of the womb? That's tough at thirty, isn't it?

Divine: It's funny when you put it that way. But, yes, awareness and fear are in opposition to the other. The soul watches as the opposing energies of living in the present or operating from the past wear you out. Back and forth, up and down, side to side. You become so exhausted that resting in the dark is more inviting than living in the light.

Seeker: Do we bring the shadow with us into the present, or do we leave it in the past?

Divine: Ego changes when it enters new possibilities. You cannot rid yourself of personality, even if you are ashamed of it. The experience of awareness allows both the emotional and psychological a place of silence. There is no uneasiness and there are no unspoken feelings in such a place.

Seeker: That's the problem, isn't it, we reject our shadows?

Divine: Yes. You also project them rather than own them. The shadow is your friend when you accept and recognize its presence in your life. You may want it hidden, but it is an important part of you. The soul knows that when you are bitten by a snake, the antidote must be applied to the site where the poison entered your body. Shadow comes with its own cure. Imagine that!

Seeker: What happens after we accept our shadow?

Divine: You allow it to exist. It is not necessary to share this acceptance with others. Only a few will understand. Ironically, self-acceptance "rubs off" on others. You don't give it away verbally as much as model it. The harder we try to *do* compassion, the more illusive it becomes. This is because compassion and self-acceptance arrive from not doing. The first step is to not practice self-loathing. This evolves into not judging others. In other words, if you feel compassion for yourself, the world benefits as you expand your compassion to others. Giving compassion to others and expecting return is an ego or shadow need. This is difficult to teach in a culture that believes that compassion is a good deed done for another. Compassion is the capacity to suffer with the self until it trickles out to the world. It is not suffering for the self, which is playing the victim or the martyr.

Seeker: Does our ego grow and change with us?

Divine: Yes. During times of fear and resistance, you inner guide takes on the form of a light. Since the shadow is threatening and scary, light becomes a form of truth in the dark. Ego's distortions may persist, but you can see and know the truth. There is a feeling of forgiveness. Tears flow. The rigidity of the personality melts from your newfound compassion. Absolving guilt is no longer the goal. The soul needs you to see your feelings and ego resistance. This is the growth of which you speak. What the heart knows (versus what the ego believes) becomes self-acceptance. You can breathe better in the truth. Others have described this experience as expanding or swelling from the inside out. Growth is knowing that this is one of the many sensations of self-love. The soul wants you to honor what you have discovered by bringing it into the mundane world of ego. Such spiritual realization fuels the wish to stay in the present.

Seeker: Is it true that the more we resist, the more intense our images of the shadow become?

Divine: Resistance stores in the body as urgency. The more you resist understanding and accepting your shadow (staying out of the body), the more you stay in your head. Once there you can think up all sorts of scary images. Remember, the soul has a vested interest in thawing your emotions. It knows your body needs warmth after the indifference of your experiences. Dark, wet, and cold form ice. Anger accompanies resistance and comes in two forms: determination directed at a goal (which is healing) and anger from blame and punishment directed inward (which lessens the self). The soul intends for you to use your anger to grow in a positive direction.

Seeker: It is confusing sometimes how our darker qualities motivate us through fear and procrastination. This is an important piece of the puzzle, isn't it?

Divine: The soul's intent for presence fosters an awareness of the paradox between divinity and shadow energy. The soul wants you to enter your body to examine unconscious shadow material. In contrast, the ego wants you to use your emotional energy to fuel a mental approach (rationalization or intellectualization) in the head. Simply put, the puzzle is discovering that healing takes place in the body. Your ego fears this because it does not realize that change is necessary to grow.

Seeker: Does the shadow ever use force to get us to go in a certain direction?

Divine: Yes, it does. The shadow uses your thoughts and emotions against you; specifically, fear and self-loathing. Substance use and addiction is often the result. Everything kept unconscious strengthens the shadow.

Seeker: Why would our shadow try to scare us into a direction we don't want to go? Is it not also our protector?

Divine: This is confusing for everybody. The shadow will mirror what the ego wants. If you have been using fear for motivation or resignation to procrastinate, the shadow will mirror this. The ego knows only patterns. The shadow doubles as protector and protagonist. It represents qualities you refuse to own, love, and take responsibility for. It also fuels your passion for acceptance, forgiveness, and entering the present. When new ego replaces old, it is the shadow that protects you in the transition.

Seeker: Why does it appear that our dark side comes out of nowhere?

Divine: Human shadow is a shape-shifter. It will change into anything it needs to help you to *see*. The purpose is to *move* you, not scare you. It may appear suddenly spike your anxiety, but also your curiosity. It surprises you only when you are not aware of its intent—to survive. The soul knows that changing your thoughts alone will not heal the past. There is a tape recording in your head that you hear as the truth. This recording contains memories of painful experiences, and old speech patterns of self-depreciation. Noting and witnessing the context of these experiences changes everything. The most obvious and important thing to remember is that shadow can work for and against you.

Seeker: We have a dual relationship with our shadow, don't we? We see it at once as a partner to be trusted and an enemy to be feared.

Divine: Yes. Its role is to pull you along (as a trusted partner) or push you along (as a feared enemy). Your shadow is with you always, even to the point of awareness. A partnership with your darker qualities grows into a respect for its power. Fear of your darker qualities creates a physical sensation in the body. It is this discomfort that causes many to deny or avoid their darker side. It is simply too scary.

Seeker: We need to examine our "mental" defenses, don't we? There is always that one skeleton in the closet, boarded and locked away, that needs our attention, right?

Divine: This is another negotiation with your darker side. It convinces you that secrets should stay secrets—you should never open the doors that hide them. The soul knows that shadow is both a hindrance and a gift. By advising you to not follow ideas and old beliefs that are "locked away" in your head, your shadow can help you focus on something deeper. Such advice leads you down to the basement—or unconscious—where it is dark, wet, and cold. The more you resist, the more the shadow will push. This is when most people want the comfort of their old thoughts. After all, thinking keeps you out of your body. The gift is that the soul will direct you to the material that needs to be converted. Understandably, most people are reluctant to stay in their bodies and go deeper.

Seeker: Trusting the journey is important when we engage our shadow, isn't it?

Divine: Of course. It is difficult to trust something formed out of violation or lost freedoms. The soul wants you to make the distinction between believing and knowing your shadow. Believing suggests that you may be stuck in distorted negative thinking. Knowing means you have faith that the opposite of these thoughts are the truth. It is normal to doubt the shadow's aims. The soul teaches that your darker side has always been responsible for taking you places you did not want to go. What you do with the experience depends on your openness to learn.

Seeker: This work almost sounds like the search for the Holy Grail, doesn't it?

Divine: Yes, the soul might say it like this: "Go down inside yourself to become aware. Once there, learn what is pulling, not just driving you. When you understand this, you can't go back to the habits of yesterday. There will be a new connection with your own divinity. It may seem scary at first, but the reward is forward movement and spiritual growth."

Intention #5

Keep the path visible when we forget it is there.

5

(E)motions

Building a bridge between the spiritual and the emotional

There is a growing consensus in the medical, science, and metaphysical communities that emotion is nothing more than energy. I have often used the image of a lone boat setting on a calm lake to get across this perspective. In this example, the lake represents a field of energy and the boat, a physical body. Left alone in this isolated place, the boat floats calmly without disturbance until it meets another. As another boat passes, it creates a wake or wave of energy that disturbs the stillness. The first boat begins to rock. This back-and-forth motion represents (e)motion, which is energy plus motion.

A stressful experience that is often described afterwards as "thick air" is another example. An individual (the first boat) and an instigator (the passing boat) create energy conditions that are so thick a knife could cut them. This is what is meant when we say that emotions are contagious. Similar conditions exist internally as well. The interaction of the two boats symbolizes thinking. In a moment of contentment, one boat sits atop the surface of its emotions (water) with a single thought. The energy of the emotions remains calm until another boat (thought) arrives. Simultaneously, a wake or wave of energy excites the stillness of the original emotions, and this travels throughout the body as a thought. If this thought is allowed to pass (is not recognized or adopted as truth), the emotions return to their original state of calmness. In contrast, if the thought is recognized or adopted as truth, the thought (boat) returns and begins to circle, sending continuous waves of energy through the water (emotions). This circular motion of thought is amplification. We have seen that the average individual thinks roughly sixty thousand thoughts a day. We can see that only a few moments (boats) of repetitive thinking need occur before our emotions would overwhelm us.

(E)motion manifests as an individual's spiritual self. The word *spiritual* here refers to the vital principle or animating force within all living things. This force affects everything around it. It is the fundamental emotional and activating principle that decides character. In essence, the spiritual state of our emotional experience reflects pleasure or dejection. This invisible force informs and animates the soul. Our individual spirits work inside a container that all of psychology would label "personality." It is created, in great part, by our parents. If the container, because of its creator's negligence, becomes deformed, we label the result a personality disorder. When we form containers within containers (compartments) internally, the split from the soul worsens and our confusion increases. The soul, spirit, or true essence of who we are takes on the shape of its owner's personality. In this image, the container or personality is not a reflection of the true self. The true self is the essence of that which is poured into the container.

Emotions play a key role in our dreams and help us heal the wounds we have accumulated. They are the driving force behind any movement we make spiritually. Such a context encourages that we learn to manage and understand what we feel. Fearing or avoiding feelings make us less available for to our own selves and to others. How do emotions inform the soul? It seems they "shock" the soul into action. This is especially true in dreams. What is this action? It seems that when the soul energizes (causes to vibrate) it tries to rid itself of hundreds of false and painful identifications from the past. The more identifications it can shed, the more "present" we become. The soul's intent is that we not only get here (to the present), but that we transcend our beginnings—that we go beyond the limits of our experience and open to our spiritual and emotional selves. Evolution dictates that we develop the ability to know, understand, and profit from our life experiences. One emotion, in particular, that makes this possible is compassion—a deep awareness of and sympathy for our own suffering. This, of course, grows into the humane quality of suffering with others.

Seeker: Do we have to learn what is giving energy to our resistance internally? Is this the role of our emotions?

Divine: It is a wonderful gift to be able to feel and observe human emotion. There is nothing that occupies more time in your thoughts. You want so desperately to simplify a quality that separates and bonds everyone and everything. Clearly, people are the most vulnerable when emoting or suffering. Some outside event throws them into a place they don't want to be, and a floodgate opens. Fear is the first emotion that comes to the surface. The rest that follow are mild in comparison. It is in these moments the soul aids the spiritual/emotional in building a bridge. You don't realize it at the time, but the soul's intervention moves you past what has happened and moves you into the spiritual. Many people get angry with the invisible, not knowing that they need it to get where they want to go—to a place of less suffering. The soul views your emotional reaction as an opportunity to bring this into your awareness.

Seeker: Are we to stop and examine our emotions before we move on? Do most of us hate transition because we don't want to take time to feel—let alone ponder—our lives?

Divine: Yes, many people fear their emotions, while some become addicted to them. The soul wants you to know that, before becoming attached to anything (a thought, a belief, or an object), feelings simply move emotions around.

Seeker: Is this what spiritual teachers mean when they say we are afraid of our own power?

Divine: Yes. Emotions can cause us to lose our footing or self-support. Many people describe the experience as a feeling that the ground has collapsed beneath their feet. Others say it feels like a cable has snapped on an elevator. Falling or failing feel the same internally.

Seeker: Many people are afraid of heights and flying. Is this the same?

Divine: Falling out of control from a high place or in a plane is scary, but the fear associated with spirituality is one of drowning in your emotions. The good news is that, though many fear this drowning, most are flapping their arms at the shallow end of the pool. Once they are aware of this, they can simply stand up and feel better. It is those people who fall into the deep end of the pool, where water and feelings are bitter cold, who have difficulty getting back to the shallow end. These individuals are so detached from their feelings that they become totally immersed in them and they feel lost. In the end, it is only their capacity to think rationally that can save them.

Seeker: Do we feel our opposites in extremes, alternating from feeling everything at once to feeling nothing at all?

Divine: It takes a lifetime to create an inner environment of coldness or total lack of feeling. But warmth can be foreign and frightening too. Not much unlike an adolescent learning about feelings for the first time, you can swing between extremes. Seeking a balance is maturing from the experience. Most won't allow themselves to grow without knowing how. Spiritual work is setting your feelings free and not worrying so much about how.

Seeker: Learning how to manage our emotions is a never ending task, isn't it?

Divine: This is true for most. You can be walking along the path of life and suddenly feel frightened. Trauma happens this way. Depending on the intensity of feelings, some describe this as similar to a river's current that can pull you under. While grabbing for higher ground or understanding for what has happened, you can barely breathe. This is an image of strong emotions. Such an underlying current, if made conscious, fosters understanding.

Seeker: Many of us find our emotions frightening but we may not know why.

Divine: Yes. It is important to understand that the ego and soul are working in opposition during such moments. Where the ego may see pitch-black, the soul will have you feel the sun on your face. You can take a breath in the sun, before going under again. The soul may impose a voice yelling for you to reach out. While the ego frightens you and tells that you can't reach help without vision, the soul encourages you to reach toward the sound. The soul knows that, if you are reaching beyond the fear of the ego, the turbulence will slow and enable your rescue.

Seeker: The opposing energy of the ego and soul's intent can be helpful then?

Divine: The opposing energy provides the friction of the human condition. The ego does not want to change. Even if it disagrees with your awareness, self-ishness wants to live. This will save you during extreme life predicaments. Spiritually, while the ego is out of breath, the soul is always seeing the larger picture. The soul keeps the path available when the ego forgets it is there.

Seeker: Can you explain how this emotional division happens?

Divine: You become walled off by false beliefs (ego) and the fueled emotions (spirit) that go with them. Your emotions become imprisoned, trapped, and compartmentalized by these outdated views. This is the driving force for spiritual work. If it were not for the soul pulling and the ego holding on, these false images would persist. The tears and passion of a divided self waters the garden of your potential. Awake, the soul guides you. It knows that, without this passion, you would freeze or drown. You have to accept these hated qualities to discover your personal truth. Emotions provide the energy while the soul offers direction.

Seeker: Does everyone have a sense of these inner forces?

Divine: Everyone has the potential, but not all are attending to the task. It isn't enough to be aware of the forces. It is also important to know what you are doing with them. The soul suggests that you decide what is fundamental to your happiness. It wants you to ponder that you are a spiritual being. Aware of the cycles of your human life, you can grow and reconnect with your emotions. Meanwhile, the ego will convince you that life is empty unless it gets constant proof and approval. Its emotions are childlike in their needs. Awareness allows an adult and soulful person to emerge.

Seeker: It seems we cannot know enough about this emotional and spiritual division.

Divine: Awareness of these inner workings is paramount to healing. While the ego is declaring your guilt, the soul wants you to discover your truth. The ego's self-loathing cancels the worth of your life experiences. The soul knows that, once you look through a lens of meaning, it is difficult to change glasses. To the ego, the burden of change is too great.

Seeker: So, the emotional and spiritual key is to get the ego working with the soul's intent?

Divine: Yes. When these qualities of the self align, it is a sacred moment. This is the soul's intent. Rather than led by the ego's tendency toward self-loathing, the soul's perspective of wholeness brings you into a place of forgiveness. Recognizing your divinity is essentially self-approval and acceptance. The boundary between rejection and acceptance becomes a path toward forgiveness. Image a stairway here and forgiveness becomes ascension. The soul wants to ensure that you will no longer accept living at the bottom of the steps.

Intention #6:

Recover intimacy to know the truest life.

6

Mastering Fear

Part One
Improvising to seek comfort and find presence

Fear is the first reaction to every negative emotion. Being afraid, anxious, or apprehensive is the core emotion we experience when we anticipate pain or danger. We feel a strong need to flee or fight. People experience their fear in degrees. Some describe it as a constant state of uneasiness. Others describe it as an unpleasant feeling of life-taking risk or harm—real or not. In any event, it is a feeling of extreme dislike for certain conditions. Internally, fear associates with losing love or being rejected by a loved one. Fear is the motivating force within the personal and collective consciousness. It is the energy behind such ego functions as judgment, criticism, protection, defense, control, and manipulation.

Seeker: What is it that has such a hold on us? Is it fear?

Divine: Don't underestimate fear—especially the fear felt by a child. But, the answer is that your ego is the center of your fear. The divine side of you is allowing—the ego side of you is fearful. It is in the allowing that divinity arrives. Your inner negotiation goes something like this:

> Ego: "You know why I am here. Just sit tight and I will discuss my demands. It will not take long."
> Divine (with a feeling of dread and knowing):"Yes, I know. But, you have been keeping me from realizing my potential for so long. I cannot allow this anymore."

Seeker: Are we trapped in this negotiation all the time?

Divine: Fear compels you to seek comfort. This takes time and emotional energy. Before you know it, so much time has passed that you become hostage to it. If this happens, it means you haven't learned yet that fear is a form of motivation. You can escape fear any time you choose—but not by looking over your shoulder, which means you would be moving through life blindly. If you look straight ahead, with your eyes forward, fear moves you through life not from it.

Seeker: How do we overcome or master these fears?

Divine: People's experiences are different, but your ability to meet the depth of your own feelings is key. People are constantly evaluating how they are doing with this. The difference between how we cope on the inside, and how we reveal our feelings on the outside is *so* varied. As you might imagine, suppressing and repressing eventually becomes depressing. The soul portrays this as a robotic existence. What is dealt with robotically on the inside shows itself on the outside as externally controlled. This creates a great deal of anger—and that energy has to go somewhere. When individuals express this anger outwardly, the world suffers. When individuals express this anger inwardly, they themselves suffer. The soul wants to transform these two dramatic expressions into a third possible form of release. It takes compassion and recognition of your own divinity for this to happen.

Seeker: So, if we are looking ahead, we can move through our fears more quickly, instead of tripping over our own feet?

Divine: Yes! The soul knows that you have experienced many ways of moving through life. Some were haphazard and ineffective. But that was before, and this is now. In the present, you can improvise. You can enter your life through experience. Rather than hide, you can listen to your heart and remember. When judgments and fears of your past decisions fade, you are moving toward spiritual maturity and away from what is chasing you.

Seeker: Is the goal to get into the present with these fears rather than staying in the past with them?

Divine: Yes. At first, the goal is awareness of truth about a particular issue. Eventually, you discover that truth causes old identifications to fade. This is the path of self-discovery. Not being afraid to let go of the person you *think* you are and simply *be* fosters an intimacy and vulnerability with the self that is foreign to many people.

Seeker: Letting go of old identifications makes us vulnerable, right?

Divine: Yes. Most try to put out the fire of transformation because they feel as if an old friend (ego) is disappearing. But, once you build and experience the passion of change, there is no going back. In fact, the more emotional you become, the more intense the heat. Some have described it as the soul's fever for healing. Opening the heart to compassion allows much-needed oxygen to cool you down. Once these images from the past melt away, you initially feel alone. There is only minimal trace pain from old ego images. Healing requires rest before you can awaken into a new place. Once there, it feels like summer internally. Healing fears of trust and intimacy bring with them the reality of your truest life.

Seeker: When we have feelings of fear and disappointment in ourselves, how can we be sure what to do next?

Divine: Choose spiritual work and you can stop being afraid. If you abandon your self, your fear and disappointment will continue.

Seeker: It seems we can move forward easily if we're not focused on the fear and discomfort of the journey.

Divine: This is true. Just remember that freeing the soul or letting go of the false self means arrival. It is an orientation, like knowing where you are by reading points on a compass. Focus implies "doing" something while getting present is about "not doing."

Seeker: Many of us try to stay forward and move in the right direction. But it is difficult to keep from getting turned around and giving up. This is an adjustment isn't it?

Divine: It is a perspective. When you feel life is the coldest, suffering will provide inner warmth. Many find it difficult to detect whether they are adjusting to their lives or simply numbing themselves. Compassion for the self is the difference. It is no coincidence that coldness over time lacks its original bite. Seeking in a storm will eventually reveal a light that gets brighter and closer. Though it seems like forever, the soul will bring you to an opening and shelter. You are never sure how this happens, but it does. Ironically, in your awareness is a "real-life" mirror in the form of a person or event. Though you may be unaware of it at first, it is this mirroring that brings you to an inner place of warmth. It is the soul teaching you that self-reflection brings you to the light of truth and safety. Eventually you discover that your light comes from this inner place. Your healing builds a fire that removes the persona (clothes) of your journey. The warmth of your emotions cooks away these ego identifications and fears. Some say it is difficult to judge if they are sick or running a fever or simply experiencing the heat of their healing. Resistance to the warmth brings suffering, while welcoming the warmth brings security. Surrendering to the moment means letting go of worry about what will happen next. The key is to become content and comfortable in this place.

Seeker: We do fear the discomfort of something new or unknown, don't we?

Divine: Yes. The soul knows you are unhappy with the old, but there is no way out except by learning and moving through your suffering. The soul teaches that you become stuck between your attitudes and beliefs. This can block your forward motion. Your confusing ideas, conflicting urges, opinions, and irrational thoughts gather together to build a maze. The soul wants you to know your inner guide, and that it will not allow you to go backwards. Freedom and self-expression are always ahead in the future.

Seeker: It is ironic how we rationalize our feelings when we are frightened. We tell ourselves that we will not have to face anything we cannot handle. It doesn't always help though, does it?

Divine: This is what you do in your head—rationalize. This is the reason to go down into the body—rather than up—to get away from these rationalizations. The soul's intent is to give you a "bird's-eye view" of your life experience—to turn you into an observer. Then you can analyze with objectivity what you know to be the truth. Rationalization is a defense against your fears.

Part Two
Witnessing and attending to pain so you can grow

There is a transcendental consciousness that lies at the root of the mind and from which the mind witnesses. It is from here that we "follow" our spiritual work. I call this function our "above observer." Whatever its description, it is the quality of the self that sees an event from a genuine and truth-filled perspective. As a form of presence, this layer of consciousness sees the whole of our lives and circumstances. A true witness is without judgment or critique. It is the ethical or contextual view of our life that often reveals meaning beyond the two-dimensional perspective of right and wrong.

Seeker: Witnessing? Does this mean getting outside our body and watching? Or, do you mean getting above our life experiences and viewing them objectively?

Divine: I mean getting above our life experiences and viewing them objectively. The ego makes spiritual work scary. Spiritual—or soul—work can appear in your dreams as a shadow—an unidentifiable entity. Emotionally, spiritual work presents as opposing energies. Negative or shadow energy contaminates your expressiveness, aggression, fear of life, fear of death, and your memories. This is a source of anxiety and makes you want to protect yourself. Dreams make what is unconscious conscious. The soul work experience starts on the inside and moves to the outside—not the other way around.

Seeker: It is difficult to look inside at that level. Most of us can barely look in the mirror. How can we do this and be less afraid?

Divine: Simply know that nothing that is in front of you is as bad as what is behind you. Also, the ego dominates when the emotional self trembles. Fear precedes spiritual development. Your emotional inner child does not know this. Divinity wants to feel its own presence. It does this by recovering childhood abilities of sensation, feeling, thought, and intuition. All join with the physical (body) for you to remember how to get here. The ego's stubborn fear of threat produces anger and blocks your arrival. The experience of these opposing energies internally is the source of much self-abuse and self-deprecation. The qualities at work are the ego, the inner child, the spirit (emotion), and the soul (context). You need to remember that the holder of the context holds the truth.

Seeker: And we want the truth, right?

Divine: That is the irony. You say you do, but, the ego's rigid and childlike perspective activates fear and anger, causing the dismissal of truth. This begins a cycle or pattern of self-blame and self-punishment. Only in hindsight do you realize that another moment has evaporated and your potential has been once again suppressed.

Seeker: What happens next?

Divine: A familiar experience—dejection. Your emotions go back to an earlier time and your fear of intimacy becomes reinforced. The combined view of your inner and outer worlds is confusing, and your view of life is a pale gray. You return to a fetal position internally, become despondent, and wait for the next cycle. Each time these opposing qualities meet, you release tension or let go. If you are paying attention, the pain of this process causes spiritual growth. If not, you become stuck.

Seeker: It sounds as if we compartmentalize all of these traits, influences, and energies. Is this accurate?

Divine: Yes, and you are more familiar with these compartments than you realize. When qualities of the self evoke pride they stand out more than others. Somehow you know that these traits and attitudes have stood the "acid test" of time. When this happens, they can openly integrate into the self and affirm. However, it is your lesser qualities that need the attention. Activating divinity means examining both. This is why you section them off internally. Intuitively, you know these traits need work, but you often lack the presence of mind to do it.

Intention: #7

Dis-member your life so you can re-member it differently.

7

Inner Images: Witnessing Spiritual Work

Taming, awakening, and guiding you to the present

Inner images are the language of the soul. Few recognize or bring these images into their conscious life. Many people say they cannot remember their dreams. Experience has taught me that the overriding interference of this memory is the ego. Rapid-eye-movement (REM) sleep dictates that dreams are occurring. The ego needs us to ignore or deny our soul's intent.

To be aware of one's inner life is to somehow be closer to our center. This awareness becomes an intimate relationship with the qualities of ego, which largely governs our sense of self. Inner images become the voice and compass that leads us toward awareness of ourselves—outside the ego. They become our record of the inner battle between ego matters and spirit.

Dreams, through imagination, force our inner images to the surface in symbols. The dreams are a visual representation of an object, event, or person understood through symbol and metaphor. The soul projects and organizes dream symbols in our minds and presents them to us as movie images projected so rapidly that the eye cannot see them. Dream images are much different from the persona or personal facade we present to the world. The soul's intent is for us to imagine and then to see the total self. The soul is the organizing principle. In a spiritual sense, dream symbols show the relationship between our inner and outer lives. Dreams portray the senses through mental pictures, sights, sounds, smells, tastes, feelings, and actions.

Seeker: Many people give up or discourage easily on the path. How might this look internally? Is this the cause of our feelings of hopelessness?

Divine: Giving up can be the cause of your feelings of hopelessness. If your external life is distant or significantly discrepant from your internal life, you feel imprisoned. The soul has many dream symbols for this. A common image is a room with brick walls. Perhaps it is lined with shelves stacked with your life experiences and decisions. The ego will examine and judge the content of these shelves. Emotionally, when you have had enough of such judgments, you will end such self-examination. The room then becomes smaller. The enduring quality of the soul is that it will teach you to navigate this room. The soul wants you to see life in its entirety. The soul promotes perspective while the ego holds onto the past. Egos are tenacious. To oppose the soul's influence, the ego or shadow may image a bottle of pills, a gun, or a needle for injecting drugs in this room. In this symbolic moment, the ego is making the volume of your inner voice louder.

Seeker: That sounds frightening. Is it difficult to seek a healthy context of life when you are consumed in this critical noise?

Divine: It can be. The echo of your inner critic becomes so loud that it drowns out the sound of any other guidance. The whole experience moves in slow motion. The ego is counting on you to be as afraid of changing as it is. Usually, you are. Taking this image further, you go to the shelves and pick up one of the items. If you do this, the ego lowers the volume. When you back away from the choices, the volume returns. This is the stuff of nightmares. The ego is trying to scare you to stay asleep, while emotionally the soul is trying to scare you awake. The soul wants you to consider dying to the old to begin the new. Nightmares are loud telephone calls from the unconscious. They intend to move you into the present—not take you out.

Seeker: When we want the old to die, is that the cause of suicidal thinking?

Divine: Yes it is, but the dreamer needs to understand in his or her waking life that such content is a metaphorical wish for death. In reality, it is an emotional need for some portion of the ego to die. Again, the ego is the source of your emotional pain. It is relentless. Its primary role (unless it is healthy) is to keep you from becoming spiritually mature or conscious. The soul wants you to live. It guides you toward ego-death so you can physically live now. Nightmares are a scream for presence.

Seeker: How do you know that you are getting better at letting go of these old images from the past? In other words, how can we tell that we are growing or healing ourselves?

Divine: Life is a progression—uncovering and recovering. Listening to your soul is a progression of dis-membering and re-membering. Once you are awake to the possibility that something larger than your ego is guiding you, everything changes.

Seeker: Can you give me an example of what this "something larger" is and how it might look internally?

Divine: The image that works for everyone is that of a "light" coming on. Essentially, as you begin the work of self-understanding, you are in the dark. At first, you are seeking the light switch. Groping in the dark, the ego will try to scare you away from it. Each time you reach for understanding or clarity (light), screams of the past may grow louder. Each time the screams fade into the distance, you flip on one switch and advance to the next switch. It is like a game of hide-and-seek, using the light to see your way for a moment, and turning it off again to move through the dark. It is no wonder you stumble along the way. At first you feel the coldness of your own emotions. Remember, guidance by the ego alone is a shallow existence. Moving to the next moment of clarity, the ego may produce new screams. This time it feels like torture to listen to. You turn off the light immediately and move again. You continue to stumble, but keep going. By this time, you are beginning to sense the warmth of your emotions. You are becoming a feeling human being again. This is evidence that you are coming alive and moving into the present. For the first time in a long time, you can feel the passion of your experience. As you become aware, listening becomes a choice. You may still be in the dark, but something is different. The ego is quiet here. As the "light" hits your eyes, you can see yourself. You are experiencing yourself as an observer. You see the contrast between being cold with death and warm with life. In fact, you see yourself coming back to life! You are consumed in the passion of your journey, and the moment is overwhelming. You switch off the light and fall to your knees. The soul's intent lets you know that you have survived. You take a deep breath, and realize that you have been asleep and lifeless a long, long time. Now, you are resting in the dark by choice. You know where the "light" is. When you are ready, you will switch it back on again. This is a beginning.

Seeker: That is wonderful! I can see the metaphor that we play hide-and-seek until we are ready for self-recovery. That is so powerful.

Divine: Yes, self-recovery is the beginning of a life full of presence. There is still the need for courage and patience though. Pealing back the veil of the ego reveals many layers—so many at times that people become discouraged. It is important to learn and practice compassion to have the confidence to push forward.

Seeker: No matter what our experience internally, the ego is constantly trying to block our path: dark versus light, cold versus warmth. Is this inner problem always there?

Divine: Yes, this is the human condition. As you move through the corridors of your inner life, the ego will produce high walls of ice. You will feel a sense of being in a maze. You can take comfort in knowing that, once it becomes aware, the soul will direct you. When you turn around, a large piece of ice may slide into an opening. This is the soul stopping you from going backwards. The ego will exaggerate the cold, while the soul wants you to honor the silence. The ego wants to scream to break the quiet. The soul teaches you to allow it. It is in this silence that you will hear your one true voice. This is the solution to the inner problem of which you speak.

Seeker: If our internal condition is a maze, what might be an inner image for ego?

Divine: As you twist and turn on the path, the ice wall blocking your direction, you may see a shadow figure through the ice wall. Tall and skinny, it will mirror your steps. This is an ego image of you. This image represents your rejected emotions and fears. The image will scare you at first. You fear rounding a corner and coming face to face with it. This quality of the ego knows you are afraid of it. It will reach to touch you by putting its hands on the ice wall. Unable to do so, it may drop to its knees. Colder and colder in this maze, you will helplessly mirror its behavior and huddle to your knees.

Seeker: So, we feel connected to this darker mirror image of ourselves? It is a reflection of sorts. How does the soul intervene here?

Divine: Yes, this shadow image is the rejected self. The soul may intervene by providing a lit candle to try to melt the wall between you and your rejected side. It is the soul that measures the distance, as well as the thickness, of the wall that stands between you and your shadow identity. It suggests that, if you apply heat directly to where your shadow huddles, it may be too close. Repressed shadow takes energy (fire) to melt defensive walls, but it isn't enough to have the need. One must bring passion or burning feelings to the work, as well as an objective distance from the opposition. You can melt the wall to enter the corridor, but it is best that you not be directly in front of the shadow. These are examples of the guiding symbols of soul.

Seeker: Objectivity is important in this work. Is this the soul's gift?

Divine: The soul acts as your above observer. It is important to allow its perspective. For example, the soul often teaches that freedom is in the opposite direction of the ego's influence. Or, staying with the "above observer" metaphor, the opposite wall. Meanwhile, the ego may pound and scratch the wall for attention. Only objective compassion can turn its ear from such an inner scream. Remember, the soul wants you to allow silence. Or, said differently, to hear the truth of your heart over the voice in your head.

Seeker: The inner voice of the ego can be deafening. How can we stand it?

Divine: Spiritual maturity comes out of silent moments. If you have ever experienced a second of inner peace, you will remember it. That memory produces hope and faith that another such moment is possible. Intolerance for this inner noise means you are coming to a melting point. Some say they feel like they will die if they don't change. When suffering reaches its peak, walls melt and barriers come down. You feel the warmth of the sun entering your life. No longer trapped in the maze, the soul offers a garden full of possibilities and growth. The sound in this place is beautiful.

Seeker: When we begin to feel better, is there is a realization of how much we have neglected ourselves?

Divine: Yes. The soul may give you an image of a garden that has withered, dried up, or is dying. The ground has cracked from the heat of your suffering. This is the image for neglect. But, the soul knows something that you have forgotten. When ice melts, water appears. It will run into your garden and bring life to everything that grows. After resting from your journey, you will awaken to see healthy flowers and plants, a soil that is moist, and a life that is fertile. Again, through the heart's perspective, the blues are bluer and the greens greener.

Intention #8

Keep on course even when it hurts.

8

Resistance

Part One
Realizing that the opposite of resistance is freedom

The Ego's natural reaction to the soul's intent is resistance. Since personality forms in the first six years of life, the ego knows only the past and has no view of the future. Its natural posture (to survive) is to oppose, disapprove, and disagree with spiritual maturity. This is a mechanical force that retards or opposes movement. It is either unresponsive or knows only one response—fear—to the unknown. Emotionally attached to the past, the ego is unwilling to bring repressed feelings into conscious awareness. The ways it can resist are countless. Most obvious is resistance to presence. Living in the now means certain death to ego illusions about the person we think we are.

Seeker: First we seek to overcome the fears of the ego. Then we discover the soul's intent. Why do we fight it so much?

Divine: Resistance is the biggest hurdle for everyone. There are many reasons people fight being present. The soul reports these top twelve ego questions:

1. Where is this leading me, and will it ever end?
2. What if I find out that I don't deserve happiness?
3. What if it has been so long that I can't change?
4. What if I am a coward?
5. What if nothing makes me happy?
6. What if I can't gain control?
7. I crave. I want. I guilt. I shame. Won't I lose it all?

8. I can't stop going in circles, and it is wearing me out. How will I go on?
9. What if I end up alone and no one wants me?
10. What if I am worthless?
11. How do I stop feeling stupid?
12. What if I can't find the real me?

Seeker: If I understand this correctly, these kinds of questions happen only when we are beginning to wake up. The light has come on and we are reevaluating our lives. Is that accurate?

Divine: Yes. You are beginning to give value to your experiences in a way you did not before. Artist Michelangelo Buonarroti describes it beautifully: "I saw the angel in the marble and carved until I set him free." This is the work of removing the prisoner from its prison—the personality. The ego tenaciously wants to keep the marble as it is to preserve status quo. This is the source of your spiritual work.

Seeker: Why is it so difficult to trust spiritual work?

Divine: Because often, when you begin to feel better, the ego will remind you of a past time when something ruined that feeling for you. The soul teaches that, when you do not allow good feelings, you experience a loss of support. Most people grow up feeling responsible for someone else's emotions. The ego uses memories of guilt or shame to rob self-appreciation.

Seeker: So we have to think outside the ego casing—the marble—to recognize that we are so much more than these weakening self-images?

Divine: Yes, the soul wants you to realize that life is a journey not an endurance test. This is the intent for wanting you aware. The soul knows your motivations, ambitions, and fears, all of which move you through life. When you are awake, these emotions contribute energy to your spiritual work. When you are asleep, you are at the mercy of the ego's influence and fate. This is the key. Before you can grow, an understanding of both realities is necessary.

Seeker: It sounds as if we need to make a shift in perspective, but the ego fights this change?

Divine: Yes, the ego wants to prevent the merging of your life experiences and will only focus on the past or future. The ego knows that you must live in the present to experience change. Thus, it will constrict you in all ways possible. The ego dislikes presence. It knows that, when the personality changes, some portion of ego dies. Becoming aware of the ego's influence is important to developing insight. When you begin to feel the release of its resistance, you feel free. This is the soul's intent.

Seeker: This releasing, is it the same as letting go?

Divine: Yes, if one gives the soul the opportunity, it will reveal what is motivating us. Our struggle with passion, anger, need, resentment, and frustration melt the ego away. Grounded in the soul's intent, we become more light and less dark.

Seeker: Holding on is our source of suffering, isn't it?

Divine: Yes, holding onto the present can cause suffering, but that suffering can transform you. By accepting the "skeletons" in your closet, you bring about a true picture of your life. This is the "fire" of suffering that transforms you. The soul knows that, if you seek long enough, there is life after skeletons.

Seeker: So, we become whatever we give our attention too?

Divine: Yes. The soul will show its intent by getting you to stay on course—even if it hurts a little. If you are honoring your instincts and valuing your experiences, the soul can guide you. This is the path to uncovering your personal truth.

Part Two
Seeing through the imaginary veil of the ego

Setting boundaries warrants respect for our personal space and integrity. For many, spiritual crisis occurs when someone allows or experiences a violation of personal space. Recovering these "lines in the sand" and fixing them as unwavering demarcations is a critical step toward healing. Many describe these violations, or the circumstances that precede them, as intellectual errors in judgment. Such is the language for the unconscious or unaware. To them, they are dealing with the unforeseen or unexpected as if blindsided by life. Living in this manner forms the trap into which the blind fall. Inner pictures for these conditions are many.

The soul's wish is that you become aware so such images become worth more than a thousand words.

Seeker: Are the pitfalls in spiritual work by design?

Divine: Getting across the ocean, through the woods, out of the pit, over the wall—these are the images of soul work. They all suggest boundaries and obstacles to overcome. The soul will bring you to these places internally again and again, until you get the message. It knows that these imaginary boundaries represent the path to self-love and forgiveness. Self-love emerges because of the soul's persistence. Such love is your birthright. It comforts and protects you from a biting ego—your own and the egos of others.

Seeker: We shouldn't force our way through these inner challenges, should we?

Divine: Trying to force an opening in this work is similar to forcing labor. You can't use force, especially since it is nothing more than the ego's impatience. Awareness and subtle allowing get you to a place of birthing. At first, the light ahead is terrifying and elusive. Over time it becomes soothing and feels safe. You cannot rush into it. Birthing has to be natural and free from the demands of ego. It is this natural allowing that provides you warmth and comfort. The soul wants you to learn this, especially in times of fear and doubt. The soul knows that, if you can set this to memory, everything will change.

Seeker: There is an urge to look back at our lives when we can't find our way. Is this going in reverse?

Divine: Yes, but only if you forget the ego is trying to block your wish for presence. Its role is to distract you with childhood memories—memories that do not fit today. In fact, there is an imaginary line between the soul and ego that represents a veil of truth. The soul wishes that you remove this veil and incorporate truth into your life. Though it doesn't seem possible, the true self is only inches away on the other side of this veil. The past, present, and future are one in this place. If you fear the truth, you will never see beyond the ego's filter. It is constantly influencing you to go back, around, or over the events in your life. There is no contentment in doing that.

Seeker: We are on a ledge between the warmth of the soul and cold of the ego. We can freeze if we make the wrong choice, right?

Divine: The soul teaches that fear comes from attaching to ego. However, fear is always behind you—from the past. Once you experience self-love, you no longer have to live in the past. The ego will scare you from freedom and truth by convincing you that it is dangerous. Keeping the past in your awareness, the ego wants you to fear failure. In fact, the soul knows that fear motivates. Fear can move you forward or backward. If you give into it, you will fall victim to its grasp and find yourself further away from your divine truth. By design, the ego makes you doubt, second-guess, and debate life solutions. This is the cold of darkness.

Seeker: Is it selfish to want to stay in the warmth of your divinity all the time?

Divine: Everything the ego decides or does is selfish. It is always about getting more of something. Just know that, when you become aware of your own significance, you are marching to the soul's pace. Imaginary boundaries exist between the cold and warmth of what you seek. These will disappear over time and become less frustrating. Past, present, and future merge. Your evidence of this is that self-loathing decreases or stops. Truth is intolerable to the ego. It cannot exist when you are feeling your own warmth.

Part Three
Choosing self-love over the ego's distractions

"Choice" can be defined as an action taken because of your own will or wish. Typically, there are many alternatives from which you can choose. Choice involves thinking about and judging the merits of these alternatives and then choosing one. Often, when we suffer, it is because we are unable to see such choices. Consumed in our emotions, we activate thoughts that blind our ability to evaluate alternatives.

In a spiritual sense, choice is deciding to renounce the ego's influence and its various distortions. By doing this, we decide to take a contextual or ethical view of our lives—inside and out. Compassion for the self is a key ingredient for such a perspective to occur. This view supports the soul's intent according to our wish for presence. Free will becomes preferential determination for things we wish for. Power means guiding our emotions to make life happen. Therefore, in order to make spiritual choices, we need to part from the old to allow room for the new.

Seeker: Much of our work involves making choices. Is this true?

Divine: Indeed, there are many choices. Internally, people have little partitions for each behavior, belief, and attitude. Some are open to change; some are closed off. Each partition represents the habits and self-images unique to a portion of the personality. As you mention, there is much duality. Even the emotional tone that fuels these images can be light or dark, positive or negative. The path to self-recovery is usually somewhere between. We move down into the dark and then up toward awareness or light. The soul's intent is to reveal that these two paths may lead to a third possibility—compromise. Our duality is a measure of the internal climate. When we are recovering divinity, the soul gives us choices. The soul knows that much of human suffering grows from a feeling of having no freedom to choose.

Seeker: This is a source of guilt for many of us, isn't it?

Divine: Yes. You can live in guilt at your own confessional or create an altar of self-love. You know you have arrived when your ego is no longer running the show. The ego can make self-love feel foreign in order to block its meaning. Allowing self-love means the ego's tricks are not working. In the end, you can choose to have a horizontal or dual relationship with the ego or a single vertical relationship with your divinity.

Intention #9

Fuel the fires of transformation.

9

Letting Go of Expectations

Hearing the ego turn up the volume; feeling the soul turn up the heat

Letting go is a virtue in spiritual practice that requires the giving up of your self to a higher plane. Letting go is surrendering to the perspective of our above observer. It is a practice of loosening the ego's grip on the self to arrive at self-realization or inner freedom. Most who aim for spiritual understanding ask *how* to let go: "What do I do?" Ironically, this experience is more about *not* doing. In other words, to experience letting go, we need only stop doing. This, in turn, allows other possibilities. Stop doing what? Usually it is clinging. Letting go of the motivating need behind whatever you're doing means to let go of outcome. Continue to act, just don't allow the need for a specific outcome to weigh on your mind.

This is more difficult than it sounds, as most of us can identify only obvious negative emotions like anger and fear. Need and clinging are much more subtle. We live in a culture that has conditioned us to control and to cling. We define ourselves by our possessions. Such an idea of ego-self is so real that it is difficult to tell illusion from reality. The soul wishes us to know that we are more than our personalities. But we cling to the "I" and "me." By letting go of these images of ourselves, we do not do anything. Rather, we uncover the gift of true essence.

Seeker: Letting go defines spiritual work, doesn't it?

Divine: Yes, and this is a difficult lesson for many to understand. It is a rare gift to be able to trust in what you feel and intuitively know it. Many of us have moments of feeling good or clarity, but we quickly cloud them in doubt. Another role of the ego is expectations. The ego tells you that, when you find what you seek, it will not be what you expect. In fact, you will be vulnerable and visible to the outside world in frightening ways. This is the fear of being seen, and the fear of never being seen—an ominous and impending reality that the ego holds over your head. The echo is that you are repulsive or otherwise not worthy of love. For some, this message lays burned on the surface of the soul. It is the ego's job to keep reminding you of this false message.

Seeker: During a moment of clarity or certainty, we often feel like something or someone is going to pull the rug out from under us. That is sad, isn't it?

Divine: It is not sad if you understand the tenacity of the ego. Remember, it has had your whole lifetime to gain dominance. Once you wake up, you have to be fully present to combat its influence. It takes time to build this confidence. Faith in what you know to be the truth is the key. While the ego turns up the volume, the soul turns up the heat. The soul's intent is to fuel the fire of transformation. The ego will make this fire feel like suffering. Locked inside this thinking, the ego taunts your need for change.

Seeker: What images might the ego use to taunt us?

Divine: Imagine lying drenched in the passion of your journey. This sounds romantic enough. The ego can take this same image and soak you in gasoline and throw matches (thoughts) at you to frighten away your romantic view. The flames of suffering and the passion of awakening are hard to distinguish at times. The soul may shift this image to the "light" of awareness, and present it to you one match at a time. Meanwhile, the ego makes you fear death by fire. This is difficult to detect without some inner wisdom of what is occurring.

Intention #10

Activate the heart's sensitivity to the divine.

10

Activating Divinity

Gaining confidence that we can feel and be better

Our divinity is the force that makes us greater than our human frailties and drama. It is a quality of being and a way of sensing our existence. The sense organ for this divinity is the human heart. It is the resting place of our feelings and intuitions. The heart's rhythmic contractions move us through life in the same way it moves blood through our body. It is the most essential and vital part of what it means to be human. The heart and soul of something is *all* there is of it. The heart's inclination or tendency is of a certain kind—a positive feeling of liking. In Christian traditions, and later literature, the heart is a metaphor that refers to the moral core of a human being. It includes both our intellect and emotions. The heart—with the brain—is mind, will, and intent. As the seat of our emotions, particularly love, the heart connects directly to the core of who we are. It is our spiritual center.

The heart's circulatory system is our power supply. The heart must beat constantly because the body's tissues—especially the brain and heart itself—depend on a constant supply of oxygen and nutrients delivered by flowing blood. Activating the heart's sensitivity to the divine is the soul's intent. As a muscular organ, the heart contracts rhythmically, around sixty times a minute, as it circulates our blood. As a sense organ, its rhythm is in direct contact with our true nature and the universe itself.

Activating divinity, then, means putting yourself "in touch" with your heart. Such an activation is an important part of the soul's journey. Though suffering puts us in touch with the heart, years of neglect can harden it and keep it from opening up. The heart is the eternal symbol of love and life force within all human beings. Getting to the "heart of the matter" suggests that the heart connects directly with truth. However, these truths can be distorted by bitterness, deception, and betrayal. In a world governed by ego and shadow, many of us today live in fear. If you get in touch with your heart, you can get out of your head and into your body.

In Buddhism, the heart is the seat of spiritual consciousness through which the higher ego acts. Activation of the heart seeks to impress the lower ego while working through our intellect. As our spiritual center, the heart makes possible the discovery and expression of love through grace, which is the physical dimension of love. Once love is revealed, individuals can choose to live there—every day. Love's journey does not occur outside the self, but inside and through the heart. Often portrayed as a doorway to soul, love opens or closes with compassion.

Seeker: Is it safe to say that awareness of our deeper inner self or wisdom is important?

Divine: Yes, without awareness, life is a never-ending marathon. Ask runners what it means to "hit the wall." They will tell you the experience is total physical, emotional, psychological, and spiritual exhaustion. Being unaware of your own pace, rhythm, endurance, heart, passion, and motivation leaves you to the mercy of the ego and external world. The soul and its divine guidance activate when you becomes aware of them. Essentially, blues become bluer and greens become greener. It is such a feeling of being alive that the outside world becomes a necessary, but secondary, concern.

Seeker: Activating our divinity sounds so beautiful. Is it as difficult as it sounds?

Divine: Is it difficult to be a part of one's own healing? It is a commitment. People worry all the time about their physical health. Most are unaware that the body remembers every emotionally painful experience that it has. It all starts and ends with the heart. Heal the heart and everything else will follow suit.

Seeker: What are we healing, exactly, when we heal the heart?

Divine: Spiritual teachers recognize that many people feel the loss or absence of their own divinity. The emotion this creates relieves itself in the abdomen or stomach. It is a wound to your true nature—a hole in the self that may create a longing for physical contact or a wish to give to others. Feeling this leak of worth at a core level decreases trust and causes people to hold back. When the natural inclination to self-express feels injured, intimacy is distorted and seems impossible to get. Because the abdomen connects with your digestive nature, physically and psychologically, people carry their dis-ease there. The soul's intent is that you heal this.

Seeker: Dis-ease? Can you explain this further?

Divine: It seems that many people fear recovering *who* they are. Dis-ease is inner discomfort or apprehension about spiritual truths. First, people fanaticize that there is an assembly line of actions to take. Then, they think there is a right or wrong way to *take the actions.* The irony is that much of the healing happens because of what people *stop* doing. Becoming aware—discovering, and then recovering the true self—is not a pass/fail or an endurance test. Becoming aware is letting go of false images and identities rather than trying to fix them. The soul wants people to recognize their harmful self-images—then let them go. In fact, the soul mirrors the work uniquely in individual dreams. Nightmares or intense dreams are examples of inner qualities needing to die or be expelled The soul's intent is that we be aware enough to make these inner distinctions and feel guided by them. That quality of the self that fear, urgency, and panic cannot erase *is* your divinity. The challenge is to uncover it. The soul intends to wake you to this. Spiritual maturity becomes the process of developing a context of understanding for your life. This is the journey.

Seeker: So, if we allow it to happen, the soul will ground us through the experience?

Divine: Yes! The soul encourages you to have more confidence in your ability to feel better. The soul encourages you to let go of one ego identification at a time, rather than overwhelming yourself by letting go of all of them at the same time. The soul knows that to uncover your divinity is essentially one ego-death after another—a death and rebirth of the self. When ego identifications or the false-self dies, divinity lives!

Intention #11

Embrace forgiveness for its healing qualities.

11

Forgiveness and Mercy

Part One
Placing ourselves in good standing with our personal truth

Compassionate feelings foster a willingness to forgive or excuse someone for a mistake or offense. We can grant forgiveness with or without being asked. In spiritual work, teachers know that, when we can forgive ourselves, we are best able to forgive others. The virtue of forgiveness places us in direct alignment with our soul's intent. Like love, forgiveness is a physical state of being. It holds us in good standing with ourselves. We are fully acceptable and comfortable in our own skin.

Seeker: So, having the soul's context is important? If we ignore its wisdom or how the spirit (emotion) works to inform us, we have a problem?

Divine: Context from the soul's perspective is an ethical view of the self. Emotions inform the soul what and how we are thinking. Not knowing this is the problem.

Seeker: It is a constant internal battle, isn't it? It is as if we have become so familiar with being asleep that we don't know how to be happy?

Divine: It is difficult for most people to take responsibility for their own happiness. We find ourselves becoming dependent on something outside to make us happy. This prevents any serious connection with our inner divinity. If you do not have enough love for you, you will not feel worthy of someone else's love. Seek and embrace your personal truth and the soul will bring you into the present. The way to happiness is forgiveness.

Seeker: Is forgiveness letting go of resenting past wrongs?

Divine: Yes. Forgiveness is one of the most important qualities of the soul. It is also the hardest for you to practice. It is not dependent on an action. It is a condition of allowing. You allow happiness. You allow love. You allow forgiveness. It is so difficult for most because they fixate on *doing*: "I should have been able to *do* something about what happened to me."

Seeker: Is this what many teachers mean when they say you can carry your own space with you? Once you allow love to enter your life, everything changes?

Divine: Yes. The soul witnesses your life and wants you to heal whatever needs healing. It sees the problem of a guilt-driven existence fighting against forgiveness. Allowing forgiveness creates a space where you can honor the self. The soul wants you to make this space sacred.

Part Two
Combining leniency with compassion for mercy to the self

Leniency and compassion combine to form mercy, which is a disposition of kindness and forgiveness. To grant mercy is to withhold justice when justice is punitive. In other words, to not deliver a natural consequence for something judged as wrong. Spiritual seekers long for mercy and find it when they ask, "What if my self-judgments are inaccurate?"

In modern times, a mistaken identity or distortion of self is the leading cause of psychological suffering. Spiritual healing, at a fundamental level, removes self-loathing, which is a psychological condition in which individuals detest themselves so much that they become spiritually lost. When the feelings of self hate and disgust reach a certain intensity, the compulsion is to act on them. As there are only two places to go with such energy—inward and outward—when they are not attacking themselves, they are attacking others. What evolves is indifference or apathy. Their experience is an overall lack of emotion, motivation, and enthusiasm. Moderate levels of apathy become depression. Extreme levels of apathy—self-hatred—bring disassociation, lack of caring, complacency, disinterest, and anesthetization.

Self-disgust feels unacceptable, but self-disgust can be changed through compassion. When an individual suffers with the self in this manner, mercy becomes a form of grace. A disposition of generosity pointing toward the self can eventually nourish the soul. It is a soul quality or state of love that can realize mercy.

Seeker: We align ourselves with self-hatred as children and feel deserving of it, don't we?

Divine: Yes. Here you have little people believing that they are responsible for harm done to themselves. They learn to believe that must deserve it. This begins the pattern: if the children could be emotionally available to the adults in their lives, the adults might be available for the children.

Seeker: We are so innocent! This is one of those times we should be able to ask the judge for an appeal, isn't it?

Divine: The soul's intent is for you to allow this appeal yourself—to recognize your own innocence, to grant yourself mercy, to set yourself free for time served. The soul wants you to know that *you* are your own judge and jury. You are no longer at the mercy of someone else's judgments.

Seeker: We "yes but" ourselves as we approach this truth, don't we? It is almost as if we need some outside force to overthrow our own verdict. How do we get out of the ego's realm?

Divine: The ego's influence is unavoidable, but the soul's intent is that it not be the lone dominating force. If you are fully present to better parent the ego's affect, everything changes. Mercy allows that you were unable to know the truth of what was occurring. Mercy allows that caretakers did not intend for you to lose yourself during childhood. This is how mercy begins.

Part Three
Empowering ourselves to make better decisions

The goal of this book is to communicate an understanding of the soul and the interior life of the human experience; in particular, the soul's images for an individual's personal inner-scape. There is evidence that our inner negotiations with the self have a spiritual center important for human development. Our innermost, essential, and intimate ego traits take on the form of identities. These many identities, if understood and brought into awareness, provide us with a unique inner wisdom. Combined with our inner authority, these same images hold the power of spiritual life or death and the choices of fear or love. This unique perspective of the ego is our personal inner expert. Formed from experience and wanting to stay in the present, its decisions and views can be definitive. However, earlier ego distortions from personal and cultural conditioning do not guarantee pure healthy decision making. The soul's intent is for us to make our inner authority sympathetic to healing, and less susceptible to influences from the past.

Seeker: Is our internal authority unique to our gender?

Divine: Symbolically, authority is strong while receptivity is gentle. You can see the difficulty: one is power and the other openness. So yes, for many the opposite gender is where the work is. This means men work on resolving issues with their mothers, and women, with their fathers. Of course, it can be the other way around. In the end, these two qualities continually want to integrate internally. Fairy tales present this as the prince and princess or as the divine marriage. It is the soul that wants this marriage or synthesis to occur. The soul knows the divinity you seek is within you and attainable. It is there for the finding, in every moment. Blinded by ego, you find that your self-perceptions remain false and outdated. The soul prompts you to let these images go, while the ego dares you to try. Because there is always some fear in a dare, many people are stopped in their tracks.

Intention #12

Keep from straying too far from an image of wholeness.

12

Truth and Hidden Influences

Understanding that we need not know how to be because there is a model for wholeness in the soul's memory

Many think of truth as verifiable facts or a quality of being near to a true perspective. Physics, however, avoids such a qualification except to speak of truth in estimations. Religion speaks of truth in absolutes, most of which cause confusion or misunderstanding among its followers. In fact, many spiritual seekers feel religious absolutes give little comfort during times of suffering. The soul's intent is for us to experience presence and the love innately available in the physical dimension of truth. Presence disallows self-deception and washes away ego delusions. In this way, love serves truth. Truth becomes the knowledge of an external ideal that is beyond the ego's reach. We do not reach truth by doing something, we reach it by allowing.

Understanding our personal truth is difficult because it puts us in contact with internal polarities. The ego sees the world through a two-dimensional lens, and this can destroy personal truths. However, presence allows love. This places our above observer or soul in front of a three-dimensional lens. This broader experience of reality recognizes a connection with a larger source. Inner dualities present as one, rather than as conflicting opposites, which creates a third possibility. Said differently, one plus one equals three. This realization is an experience of truth.

Truth is the most acceptable understanding of reality that an individual's mind or reason can make accessible. It is outside reason and mind, and is in a realm most call metaphysical. Truth is what the soul sees. Nothing makes this clearer than viewing and grasping our dreams. Such an examination of our inner life reveals a working context for truth, whether we understand it or not. Context, from the soul's perspective, is congruency. When a person's inner and outer lives are incongruent, personal truth is distant. This distance produces fear, anger, and, eventually, depression. In contrast, when a person's inner and outer lives are suitable, there is balance and a conformity to the soul's intent. A person who has discovered a divine standard experiences genuineness or authenticity. Living spiritually in this place guarantees a life full of subjective revelation and faith.

Truth is self-evident when governed by an internal and ethical principle. Self-judgments no longer do great harm; neither can they be dispensed at random by the ego. There is no right or wrong way to exist. We can simply *be* real and the person our soul intended us to be. This way, we experience a quality or state of being true. We do not evangelize this truth to others as if it is an absolute truth. Rather, a personal truth—as a physical place—is a path to awakening. There is enough evidence by spiritual sages that a lone seeker who finds his or her way can change the world. We can get into trouble when we take that person's private experience and define it as "the only way" for all of us. Though all roads lead to the same place, we all still have to travel our own individual path to meaning. True-ness is determined by our own journeys on our own paths. Someone else cannot take this journey for us. Religious and spiritual camps separate on this point.

The ego is a powerful, unconscious influence in our search for our true selves. The ego often tells us that reality is in our views and opinions, but it is the soul that intends for us to learn our personal absolutes—internally. Disguised or repressed, these absolutes are most visible in our dream symbols. Our ego hides from us our true essence. Once we become aware of this, everything changes.

Seeker: There is a force or energy behind our movement, isn't there? We can sense this force but may not always see it. Is the leftover debris from our choices the cause for our doubt?

Divine: Yes. You must observe and understand hidden forces and influences through your senses. If you listen to these influences instead of fearing them, they will move you toward the soul's intent. But, as we have learned, the ego resists such movement.

Seeker: Can you explain this force further?

Divine: The soul's energy wants you to move in a specific direction. Initially, it may be toward an imaginary cave or outcropping of rocks. This is its image for your internal forest. Rocks represent reality and the eternal, while caves symbolize the womb. The soul knows that you will try to resist because the ego fears life.

Essentially, internal work is death and rebirth. The soul's intent is to move you toward life. If you allow it, the soul's images will teach you the difference between the ego's illusions and reality.

Seeker: Is the soul pushing us toward ego death?

Divine: Yes, the soul pushes us toward the death of ego's illusions. Imagine a forest floor covered with hundreds and thousands of snakes of every shape and size. Though they are frighteningly close to you, they move toward an opening in a cave. You are afraid because everything seems so dark. In truth, there is light coming from a slit in the cave wall. Though you are stunned by what you see, the soul wants you to stay calm, watch, and hold this image in your imagination. If you do not, fear will cause it to disappear and you will be lost again. This is the pattern for many.

Seeker: This is an example of awareness or presence, isn't it? The soul wants us to see and hold the image of the light, despite the dark?

Divine: Yes, yes. It is during such observations that a friend, confident, teacher, or mentor is useful—someone who can hold your hand as you wake up for the first time. Most need convincing that the light is real. Many people describe ego fear as biting or engulfing. In these moments, it is natural to reach for safety.

Seeker: Descriptors such as "sinking" and "suffocating" come to mind.

Divine: Yes. You don't realize that when you are making direct contact with the force. You fear that that force is actually life's energy. Allowing and cooperating with its intended direction will move you through it. Resisting reminds you of feeling helpless or alone.

Seeker: Can you explain why we struggle with the truth?

Divine: It seems many of you feel guilty and ashamed for being the person you are. There is a battle occurring internally. Unaware of its effect, you think it is your fault. You don't realize that this is the human condition—the battle of opposites. Many of you have felt empty for so long the idea of being full is foreign to you. The soul's intent is for you to realize that you do not have to "know how" to be happy. Rather, all you have to do is to allow joy into your life. Happiness for most depends on someone else's acknowledgment or approval. The soul wants you to provoke your own happiness. You don't need permission. Living mindfully is a choice. Because we are all born into grace, divinity and happiness await us.

Seeker: Is the soul's intent universal?

Divine: The soul is your connection to the source, what you might call God, or higher consciousness. Embedded in its memory is a model for wholeness. If we understand our individual design, the design of the collective simultaneously comes into awareness. Suffering comes from feeling separated from this source.

Seeker: The division is ego versus spirit, physical versus nonphysical?

Divine: Yes. You live simultaneously in two worlds—one of your ego and one of your nature. It is not your task to remove your nature from your ego. Rather, it is your task to hold onto your nature despite your ego. The ego is the dark that light or consciousness comes out of. The dark serves this purpose in the same way that death causes us to appreciate life. Our nature is divine.

Seeker: It is as if we are each on a boat in the ocean, adrift and alone. When the wind dies down and the boat stops, what are we to do?

Divine: Yes, you are on a journey on the sea of life. The soul oversees how you are meeting the rough and smooth of your life experiences. No matter how little energy you have, or how small you may feel, the soul knows how far you are from your personal shore or ground. Hidden influences can prevent your movement.

Seeker: Does the soul usually advise us when we are in such a place? It seems the light never gets any closer even though we are rowing with everything we've got.

Divine: Yes. The soul knows when you need to place yourself in a new direction. It knows that, when you do this, old influences, ideas, and views will fade. You may feel lonely, but the soul knows you can go beyond ego boundaries of fear. The ego rocks the boat and pushes you away from where you know you should be. The soul presents the light you seek off in the distance. It is this light that warms you, fosters life-giving energy, and affirms your chosen direction. This is difficult to see at first, but effort here is not as important as attending and allowing.

Seeker: This sounds like a scary time. Dark skies and rough waters can push us farther away from what we seek. I imagine the boat feels as if it might overturn and we will fall out.

Divine: Yes. Emotions will always arise that can push you further away from your task. However, these same emotions can also bring you to the brink of awakening. The fear of losing everything is the wake-up call. Fear motivates because you experience the warmth of a new direction. This is the benefit of suffering awake versus asleep.

Intention #13

Ease up on moral ultimatums and allow an ethic of self-love.

13

Patience

Accepting that anything less than patience fuels self-loathing

There is no virtue or quality more important during spiritual work than patience. It is the ability to put up with pain, troubles, difficulties, and hardship without abandoning the journey of self-recovery. It is also the ability and willingness to wait a long time for that random-variable-intermittent reinforcement (love) that comes from what we seek.

The natural reaction to impatience is anger. An essential ingredient in spiritual work, patience is in conflict with a modern culture that continually expects immediate satisfaction. The growth that comes from spiritual work requires an "as-long-as-it-takes" perspective before we begin to feel it happening. Individuals who have patience have the capacity to endure inconvenience, to highlight calmness and self-control, and are willing to tolerate delay. The spiritual opposite of patience is weakness. Having a sense of humor about life is another important quality that accompanies patience. Faith is the reward for patience.

Seeker: There have been times when I have experienced the warmth of my own divinity, but then I have lost it. Why does this happen? Is this falling backwards?

Divine: Ironically, you are not falling backwards but experiencing the ego's lack of patience. The force of frustration works against the soul's intent. You can never lose it. In fact, the void we all feel symbolizes our divinity buried under suffering and negative self-images. The light pulls and the soul pushes; this is the energy + motion—or (e)motion—of the spirit. You use the word "I" in your question. Know that "I" is the voice of the ego. Only "I" gets cold, lost, locked out, can't stop doing, can't find its way, and moves in reverse. *You* on the other hand, have the freedom of choice. Free will allows discovery of your divinity and connection with the source, your soul's love, your own significance. This is possible through the warmth of compassion. It is impossible to ignore. Many people in history have asked "Why?" The soul wants you to remember—you *will* the answer.

Seeker: When we find a place internally that reflects our passion, we somehow lose the heat of it. How does this happen?

Divine: Rediscovered passion initially lacks the fresh air of the present. Essentially, it has no experience with "now." Exhausted from your spiritual work, you will eventually need rest. This resting period allows the ego to enter, and the freshness of your discovery becomes cold. Light turns to dark, and you scream for the ego's intrusion. The ego needs you to close yourself off or block receptivity. It needs you to lose patience. Some people describe this time as feeling like winter in the middle of summer.

Seeker: Are these contradictions common?

Divine: As we uncover repressed passion, we have to cope with aloneness. The word *alone* comes from two words: *all* and *one*. For most, aloneness occurs in midlife, a time when they are above earlier ego concerns. Midlife becomes an opportunity to "open" and cool potentially painful or hot emotions. Tired from the journey, many prefer to stay unaware of these experiences. However, if you are a seeker, spiritual work does not allow this avoidance. Looking inward, you awaken to something that feels painful but familiar. The mood that accompanies this discovery can be cold as we remember old fears and repressed emotions. This begins the contraction. In this place, many say: "It feels as if it is snowing in the middle of summer." Patience during this time is important if you are to get the worth of your suffering.

Seeker: Can you explain what it means for the personality to turn against itself?

Divine: The ego's lack of patience fuels self-loathing. The ego's emotional experiences and related pain go as far back as the womb. There are multiple opportunities for the ego to turn on itself. Spiritual work suggests you are looking for resolution; the ego can become stuck in the maze of it all. Each individual has hundreds of false images of the self to release. The coldness of this examination can be intense. Impatience encourages self-attack. Emotionally and spiritually, seekers want a more intimate relationship with the self. This relationship begins with caretakers and later is internalized as "the way." The ego has difficulty waiting for and re-experiencing this.

Seeker: Intimacy is a core issue that begins when we are little?

Divine: Yes it is. Depending on where you are in spiritual recovery, the soul may depict childhood intimacy traits as numb or cold. Remember, internally unresolved passion affects anything that will burn. As children, we may be unconscious of the effects our parents have on us, but, as adults, many of us suffer from the memories of our parents' behavior toward us. In the present, the tendency is to try to convert our complacency into action. This means confronting ourselves and the past. Though the intent is to feel better, it hurts first. Once again, the soul encourages patience. It knows earlier childhood self-images will burn as easily as paper once you become compassionately present.

Seeker: It seems that, as we do this work, layers peel away and we can become stuck. Some have a hard time telling real from fantasy. It feels as if we are thawing out. Is that accurate?

Divine: The soul's image for buried feelings is coldness. Feelings generated by presence can become a strong flame of recovery. People often feel that showing or revealing emotions is negative or a sign of weakness. In fact, emoting releases energy. Personal suffering comes from passion denied or feelings repressed. Fortunately, spiritual work can "thaw" us into the present. Again, its takes patience to wait for ice to melt.

Seeker: Many people become detached from their feelings early in life. Is this the beginning of coldness?

Divine: Absolutely. No one wants to detach. It is a choice made in self-defense. Sadly, letting go of this identification is difficult. The coldness people develop as children is usually a necessary defense from the cold around them. They use the coldness as a coat to stay warm. This coat is a defense mechanism. The problem emerges when we wear that same coat in the heat of summer. It doesn't fit. Many people believe the world is cold and cruel. Also, that it is best to stay cold to live in it. This is not the soul's true essence; it is the ego's view. The world is not cruel or kind—it is both. Spiritual work is seeing the world for this truth and allowing the third possibility—love. Love prevails despite the ego's perception. It has physical dimensions both in and around us. We only have to awaken to live in it. Impatience is the ego's ultimatum to pick one side of the equation, which disallows the third and invisible possibility of love.

Seeker: There are so many choices to make during spiritual work. How do you know when you are making the right ones?

Divine: Spiritual work is having the patience for and awareness of the struggle between ego and the soul's intent. The ego would have you believe that your thoughts and life stay fixed or rigid. This discounts your spirit, or emotions, and removes free will. The key is to make your choices with your heart and not your eyes. There will be few errors this way. You know when the heart's involved because your feelings will offer feedback about your decisions. This is an importance reason to stay in touch with feelings.

Seeker: Why do so few of us feel free?

Divine: Largely we don't feel free because the ego is judging, sentencing, shaming, and rejecting the self endlessly. All of this takes place while you are aging in years, but not in maturity. You are a slave to the past. The ego is tenacious about *not* wanting this to change. While you are appealing to its authority, the soul offers two alternatives: one, you can abandon the spiritual lessons that have come from your life, or, two, you can birth a new life from the labor of your experiences. It is easy to imagine the soul's wish. Impatience abandons, while patience continues.

Seeker: So, it gets down to the fact that we have a choice?

Divine: Yes. The soul wants you to make a distinction between the past and present. You can *now* do what you wished for in the beginning. Remember, the soul offers us a context for a whole life when it creates internal characters, experiences, and feelings that wake you up. If you have the patience to see the signs, they will set you free.

Seeker: It seems we are moving forward in life until we turn our backs on ourselves.

Divine: This is the only way to be out of God's view—when you turn away from you. The soul wants you to understand that emotional coldness comes out of the past. This can make life hard today. Walk into the sun and eventually it will warm you. Turn away, and you lose yourself in the cold. Remember, patience's reward is faith.

Seeker: Is it safe to say that, the longer we can move forward, with fewer lapses in judgment, the better we will grow?

Divine: It is best to keep your eyes forward to see the truth. It is in front of you. When you are looking over your shoulder at the past, you are blind to it. Life is not an endurance test. If this were so, everyone would eventually run out of energy. Love is eternal and so are you. Growth comes when you add your heart to the seeing. Patience comes from your heart's perspective.

Seeker: Is adjusting to the cold a form of acceptance and forgiveness? It seems that, if you forgive and accept your choices, you move forward and the past loses its influence.

Divine: Yes! Adjustment is adapting. Adapting is accepting. Accepting is forgiving. Forgiving is loving. Not only does the past no longer provide the storm, but you now have a closet full of umbrellas, raincoats, gloves, and earmuffs, to wear as you *play* in the winter of *your* present. Isn't that wonderful? This is the reward of patience.

Seeker: Does having our eyes forward keep us from falling off the path?

Divine: Yes, it does. Even though you may need to shield yourself from the weather of circumstances, foresight is essential. The soul wants you to learn that, even when you walk into a storm, there is a brief glimpse of a light in the distance. It will guide you to your destination.

Seeker: So, spiritual growth happens when we move forward in the storm for longer and longer periods of time? Never losing sight of what is pulling us?

Divine: Yes, when a storm lifts, your vision improves. Adjusting to the cold of your experiences represents self-acceptance and forgiveness. This form of patience with your life equals compassion. It heals, reinforces, and provides spiritual growth each time you apply it. The opposite—impatience—makes you focus on fear and discomfort.

Intention #14

Learn lessons from life that bring us closer to truth and presence.

14

Things Happen for a Reason

Part One
Aligning our inner and outer worlds with meaningful coincidence

"Things happen for a reason" is a common phrase in our culture. It's used to explain or cope with events that are seemingly out of our control. Though such events can be both positive and negative, the phrase usually follows a negative event. There is a second part to this statement that usually remains out of our awareness: "Things happen for a reason—until we 'get' it!" The implication is that, if we "get" it (the lesson), things will stop happening, and we'll be able to move to the next level. Sadly, most do not view their lives in such a way. "Things happen for a reason" implies that life occurs by fate or random chance: everything is in God's hands and who are we to question God? Life from this perspective disallows choice and wish.

Spiritual seekers wish their lives to have meaning; they welcome the lessons of life. Insights that change because of information gained by paying attention to outside events are valuable and rarely ignored. Carl Jung defined these events as synchronicity: "… a meaningful coincidence or correspondence of two or more outer and inner events. It signifies the meaningful concurrence of a physical and a psychic event which are connected not causally but by meaning."

The soul intends for us is to "get" these meanings as they will bring us closer to truth and presence. If multiple coincidental events occur (internally and externally) and we miss their meaning, we are asleep in our lives. In dreams, these events (if missed often enough) will present as nightmares. Said differently, if guidance by our dreams goes unattended, the dream will intensify. The dream is similar to a long-distance phone call from the unconscious in which the ring becomes louder if we do not pick up the receiver. These events occur in our external life as well. Wrong turns, blind decisions, confused thinking all throw us into conditions we would otherwise avoid. Once there, we ask ourselves why or how this happened. The soul's intent is for us to change our actions or to recognize a particular pattern of behavior—to get it! If we do not, events will repeat over and over until they reach nightmarish proportions.

Seeker: Do things happen for a reason?

Divine: Remember, for every experience that you have that feeds your doubts, the spirit has one that nourishes your soul. Live in the present, and such signs are all around you. You are more than the sum total of your experiences. You are the one who is having the experiences. In this way, life happens for a reason. Examine the lesson of the experience.

Seeker: Can you give an example that would make this easier to understand?

Divine: The soul intends you to find meaning and purpose in your life. The answers you get from the questions you ask are the reasons for your life. For example, imagine your life is in a small sailboat. You and some other adults are the only passengers; each of you has a private cabin. Far from shore, the wind dies and the boat stops. Through the walls of your cabin you can hear a debate going on. Some of the people are arguing that your presence has become an inconvenience. You can't believe it, but they are voting about what to do with you. These are the conditions when you go to sleep that night. When you awake, you find yourself alone in a small rowboat. They have left you behind! You think, "This is abandonment!" The small boat tosses and rocks in the experience. Alone and afraid, you do not know which direction to follow. Soon, it becomes dark. You ask, "How could this have happened to me?" Suddenly you see a big light off in the distance. Moving in its direction, you see buoys that have small lights on them. Each time you work your way toward a small light, you find something there you need. First, there is a blanket to warm you. Second, there is water for drinking. Third, there is a map to show you the way. These are the lights of purpose: awareness and presence. The buoys are working together to get you where you need to go. You now have a purpose. Life is happening for a reason. You are experiencing your own divinity—you are learning the soul's intent. A deep realization occurs. The big, distant light never gets any closer when you row toward it. The buoys between you and it are essentially invisible until you see them. The distant light and you connect to each other. Now when the sky darkens and your emotions take over, you can calm yourself by remembering. When the sea of life is rough, presence will bring you what you need. You and the light are one. You will never feel alone again. In this way, life happens for a reason. The reason: to remove the myth that you and divinity are separate.

Part Two
Realizing that true nature is recovered through vulnerability

What is a person's true nature? Nature is who we were (essence) before we were shaped by our personality and culture. The personality is an essential mixture of qualities or characteristics by which we identify ourselves. It is a causal agent that creates and controls our daily external reality. The world sees or accounts for our personality. In truth, it is a complexity of emotional and intellectual qualities that decides our actions and reactions. In fact, true nature displays as energy in its essential form. True nature represents innate behavior that is not learned or influenced by the environment. This is our true essence. Nature is inner forces in the human condition.

Seeker: What are some of the ways we block the view of our true nature?

Divine: The ways are legend. Imagine all the ways the soul has witnessed you come undone in your pursuit of freedom, love, truth, and peace. How many seconds are in a minute, minutes in an hour, hours in a day, days in a year, years in a decade, and decades in a century? It is that many ways. For example, when people view their wishes and hopes as too lofty, the soul knows it is a person's own inner authority (or lack of it) that blocks their path. Emotions, anxieties, and beliefs associated with the past capture or victimize most people today. The soul teaches you to experience this as a loss of power and vulnerability. This is why few search for personal truths. It takes courage to move forward and trust the art of becoming.

Intention #15

*Recover a crisp awareness of one's self in the world
... a subjective measure of being here* now.

15

Presence

Part One
Observing the play of thoughts, feelings, hopes, and fears

Much is written about how important "presence" is in spiritual work. Presence is the personal nature of our consciousness, separate from our ego, that is experientially knowable. It is one true way to feel our existence. Another form of presence is an "in-the-body" experience that is away from the chatter of our heads. In "absence," we are consumed in our thoughts of past worries or about the future. Presence has an invisible spiritual quality about it that's felt as a crisp awareness of one's self in the world. When we are fully here, the blues are bluer and the greens greener. Presence is a quality of the true self—a quality of our existence that comes with a willingness to be met and known. Eventually, our own presence makes us available to the presence of others. Finally, presence is a subjective measure of our emotional sense of "being here" in the world.

Seeker: Living in the present is important isn't it?

Divine: When you are learning and growing, your divinity activates. Being present makes this possible. Though the soul is always working on synthesis, emotionally you are dealing with your aloneness and your dependence on the world. Much of this work is deep and unconscious. The discovery is that many of your behavior patterns evolve from parental conditioning. The work is a process of merging your inner and outer experiences. The soul knows you must be receptive to get here, and presence fosters receptivity.

Seeker: I am sure there are many advantages to presence. There are enough books written about it. Can you expand on that?

Divine: From the vantage point of the soul, you are viewing the "play" of your thoughts, feelings, hopes, fears, and fantasies. There is no way to see the drama without getting above it. To understand your inner journey, you must see how it mirrors externally. This is how you stay aware of your progress. Activating your above observer requires presence.

Seeker: Is the above observer a larger, nonjudgmental aspect of the self?

Divine: Yes, it is separate from the ego's judgments, but is experientially knowable. This observer is a larger aspect that views all your existence. Many talk about living in the "now." Self-examination makes this possible. There is a hunger for the sensation that accompanies presence, but there is also fear. This is largely because presence prevents self-deception. The tricks and projections of the ego do not work when you are present. This is the soul's intent, getting you here despite the opposing energy of the ego.

Seeker: Can you give a simple example of how the soul's intent and the ego's opposition work?

Divine: The easiest way to portray this struggle is to image a negotiation taking place within you. On one side are the fear and emotion of a child, on the other, the wisdom and depth of your experiences.

> The child speaks first: "I have asked this before but, I want to live in the present! I have for a longtime. You know I feel this way! If you will just tell me the price, I will gladly pay it."
> Your older wisdom responds: "Presence is already yours. I can show you how this is so. But be forewarned, once here you cannot go back to the past. You cannot change your mind or find new ways to manipulate. So—do we have a deal?"
> Your childhood fears answer: "I can't go back at all? What if I need too? I don't know if I can live in the present all the time."
> Wisdom replies: "See, it is not wisdom that stops your wishes. It is you. The decision has always been yours to make."

Seeker: That seems like a no-brainer. If our pain is in the past, wouldn't we want to stop going there?

Divine: Oh, it is not because you don't want to honor the present. So many of you stay consumed by ego externals like work, family, relationships, that self-healing seems impossible. There is a lesson here: giving the ego everything it wants does little to heal the heart or fuel the soul. Constantly trying to satisfy the ego distracts you from arriving. Ironic, isn't it? Externals bring happiness, while attending to the soul brings joy. One is temporary and seems easier, the other is lasting but difficult. This is the spiritual path. Indulging the ego can overshadow the patience needed to continue spiritual work.

Part Two
Intuitively healing and restoring the soul to its original state

Intuition is a thought or feeling that is spontaneously prompted by a natural tendency. Subconscious and reflexive, intuition reveals a pattern from the parts of something. Realized immediately by the mind, it is an instinctive knowledge or feeling. Spiritually, this occurs when we see continuity in our life story. Events and experiences that seemed unrelated take shape to form a life that seems built by design. Intuitive healing is a form of understanding that eventually restores the soul to its original state. In this context, suffering is a therapeutic agent by which the soul repairs itself. In the life of a spiritual individual, soul healing is self-acceptance.

Healing in the seeker involves repairing a physical or emotional hurt. Empowered to put things right, the seeker can care for him- or herself in ways not thought possible before. Restoration follows and has a quality that the seeker describes as wholeness or balance. Today's psychics would say that this individual has achieved a higher rate of vibration and state of consciousness. Because everything is energy, someone transformed can, with intent, channel this energy to another. To heal is to reenergize and relax another.

Seeker: How do we open ourselves to or honor our intuition?

Divine: First, you must decide you want to heal. After you make that decision, you are susceptible to the soul's intent. You then must trust where the soul is taking you. You will have some struggle to stay in contact with it. Apprehension and fear are normal reactions to this. Trust and look within. This creates a place for synthesis and creativity to exist. It is then that you will find the solutions to your opposites. Creating these conditions internally makes you aware of the vast potential that is yours for the asking.

Seeker: Yes, but is there a particular way, method, place, or action we can employ to develop our intuition?

Divine: For many, intuitive healing begins with the fear of intimacy. The soul sees from its vantage point various mood states that are in need of repair. For example, the mood for damaged intimacy is often gray or dark. It may be a memory of abandonment or rejection. Old thoughts of the experience fuel your emotions or spirit. The soul may bring you to this realization countless times to wake you up to its need for repair.

Intention #16

Continue so you can continue.

16

Movement and Rebirth

Part One
Reviving learning, culture conversion, and spiritual awakening.

One of the features that distinguishes Middle Eastern religions (Judaism, Christianity, and Islam) from the Indian religions (most notably Hinduism and Buddhism) is the view of life and death. In this book we speak of rebirth as a spiritual awakening from the past into the present rather than a physical birth into the world. Healing occurs when the soul arrives with its original intent, after transcending past conditioning and distortions of the self. This new cycle of life becomes a revival of learning and culture change.

Spiritual growth mirrors the labor and delivery of a physical birth. The process begins with conception or awakening. It is an organized attempt by the soul to integrate the separated parts of a human being. Seekers use descriptors such as being pulled, pushed, or tugged during the experience.

Spiritual awakening culminates as a life lived asleep. What emerges is an "inner child" who is no older than adolescence. The reward for the work is wisdom. Many describe this as a rebirth of their life. It is no surprise, then, that this spiritual birthing better prepares them for their eventual physical death. Life lived "awake" has become richer than they imagined.

Seeker: Once we recognize that we are not separate from our soul's intent or God, does the work get easier? We peel layers, examine patterns, experience cycles. Does it ever stop?

Divine: It becomes less frightening. But, does life and death ever stop? Is this not our reality everyday? The answer to part of your question is that we continue so we can continue. Each cycle brings us closer to the divine. There is less distance between us and the light. It is the experience of change that reminds us that we are here.

Seeker: I know what a physical birth looks like, but can you give an example of a spiritual birth?

Divine: Of course, spiritual births are unique to each individual's journey, but I will try. Imagine a forest that is overgrown with bushes and weeds. There are snakes all around that you can hear but not see. You are trying to find your way, but afraid to take a step because you cannot see the forest floor. Like many people, you are afraid of snakes. Each time you think you have found a safe place to put your feet, the leaves and debris of the forest floor move. This causes you to take a step backwards. It becomes clear that you are to obey the directing snakes. They are moving you toward a cave.

Seeker: Snakes represent our life force. If we allow this inner image to guide us, we arrive. Is that what is happening spiritually?

Divine: Exactly. These images symbolize how the soul may push you in a particular direction. The cave represents the birth canal. If this presents in your dreams, birth is occurring in your spiritual work. The soul may nudge you farther along. This time, the forest may have rock formations and caves, but no snakes. The soul is assuring you now that you are aware of what is happening. Fear is no longer needed to move you. Rocks represent a boundary that, if you cross them, will prevent anything from harming you. Of course, the soul wants you to cross over, but it is your choice.

Seeker: So, birth in this image is passing through a boundary? That fits the birthing experience!

Divine: Yes, the soul may create an image of a pile or wall of rocks in which there is an opening or slit through which light can pass. People have experienced this light as warm and soothing. Even if they feel the snakebites of their past, in this place they are immune to them. Though the bites still hurt or cause fear, the light gives them something else to focus on. Awakened for the first time, most individuals cannot take their eyes away from what this opening represents.

Seeker: We are only inches away from moving through to a new place?

Divine: Spiritual awakening occurs because of the forces of your evolutionary journey. When people get this far in their spiritual work, they are inches away from experiencing their own divinity.

Part Two
Taking the steps to personal and spiritual growth

Personal growth and spiritual growth affect us intimately. When we continue this growth, our character, personality, and behavior change. Such growth prepares us for our soul's intent. Once aware of this, we experience a spiritual unfolding of events that changes us from an ego-driven life to one that is more meaningful. Some have described spiritual growth as a process of becoming significant in an otherwise tiny existence. I believe it means that we can begin to come forth, take part, and be present. Emergence of the true self makes this possible. The upside of personal growth is that it improves our understanding of things. The downside is that it may add to our confusion. True seekers are stimulated by such life mysteries. Their curiosity becomes the force that drives their work, while fear exhausts or slows their progress.

Personal growth can occur in tiny steps or in sequential jumps. Once it begins, the soul's intent is for us to grow exponentially. It wishes for the depth of our experiences to be in direct proportion to the quality of our life.

Seeker: Is there a critical first step in spiritual development?

Divine: Yes. The first step in spiritual development is understanding the purpose for your suffering and the shadow it creates. If not for shadow, most of us would give up or quit the process. The shadow provides the energy or emotion for movement. It causes you to feel your passion (suffering) and melts through various false identities.

Seeker: You speak of going down or getting above something, is this how our growth evolves?

Divine: To discover your divinity, you have to look within (down) before you can move up. Having some sense of what needs your attention is the key. Remember, you hide or bury certain qualities for fear of their exposure. Understanding the strong emotions attached to this fear is the beginning of your growth.

Seeker: Can you offer an example of this perspective?

Divine: As many of you move up the steps of transition, you can see the changes in your life. Essentially, your internal and external worlds align themselves. The abyss or void is no longer dark, but well lit by your awareness. Though it may now be difficult to see down clearly, what is clear is that you are no longer looking at the world through the eyes of a frightened child. This past perspective was narrow, needed blinders, and was fueled your apprehension. You know that your divinity is activated when transition transforms into an open or broader view.

Seeker: When are we ready for such awareness?

Divine: Many of your own sages feel that you are not ready for this self-examination until you reach midlife. Of course, there is no age limit to when you can learn from your suffering. Descending to the bottom is the norm. This is the home of your clutter—old attitudes and habits. Though it feels safe there, it is not real safety.

Seeker: Can you give an example of what it means to "look within" or "within the depths" of who we are? How might the soul make this happen?

Divine: The soul uses images for this process. Imagine you are standing at the top step of a basement. The light at the bottom is bright enough to reveal several large boxes scattered on the basement floor. As you try to identify them, the stairs begin to shorten. The light hanging from the ceiling starts to flicker. As you move down the steps to tighten the lightbulb, the movement of the stairs stops. When you return to the top step, the movement starts again. The soul is teaching that as long as you are descending the stairs, they will remain in place for you. If you stop or change direction, they will disappear at a faster pace. The soul wants you to move into this place. The lightbulb represents the awareness needed to see.

Seeker: We don't want to look within or go all the way down, do we?

Divine: When your emotions send signals to the soul, the human spirit's motivation is clear. It may be frightening, but it is clear. To recover your life, you must move through this inner universe. It is the force that leads you to growth and change.

Seeker: There is a sacrifice, isn't there, and a feeling of being alone in this place?

Divine: Yes, the ego will scream, "I've done everything I could do. I don't like what I see. Please save me!" Who does this sound like in your culture's history?

Who screamed similar words? (Hint: The story involves a cross.) Such words of desperation speak to "the parent" long before they're spoken to God. Abandonment is the original source of your anger. It happens to everyone.

Seeker: The anger this realization produces is healthy, isn't it?

Divine: Yes. This anger comes from a broken heart. You might say or think: "I am angry at you. I was scared many times, but *now* I am angry. Take responsibility for what you have done to me! I hate you for leaving me!"

Seeker: This feels as if something inside opens and pours out. Some have described it as feeling feverish or hot.

Divine: Yes. This is the "fever" of healing—from the inside out.

Intention #17

Learn gratitude, activate grace, and use compassion to move along the path.

17

The Soul's Intent

Trusting that a visible inner light observes our emotional reactions without judgment

Seeker: Is this your intent—to get us here? Are these the feelings of arrival? First, we travel through an icy maze, survive the currents of a river, and have our vision blocked by distorted beliefs. Then we meet the shadow through a wall of ice, and finally see it as angelic. Is this the process of arrival?

Divine: Yes, of course. From your perspective, this takes a lifetime. Bumping around in the dark, you become familiar with the furniture and obstacles within your personal prison. So much so, that you are able to live and move in the dark as if the lights were on. Months and years pass. You hit your head on something, stub your toe, and scrape your knee, even cut yourself. Each time you think it is your fault. You don't know that you are seeing through a filter of ego patterns, lies, and habits. Once awareness happens and the light is on, you sense your inner life. You begin seeing with your heart. Little do you know that the soul has been your navigator. The eternal is timeless. The sensation of moving within it—from the finite to the eternal, and back—gives us a sense of inner expansion and fullness. I wish for this to become real for you. If it does, the influence or stress of simply a finite horizontal existence lessens. The vertical is the physical dimension of love.

Seeker: We get to a place where you give us a choice, don't we? Initially, life presents us with tasks to do. Or, we fall into something rather than enter on purpose. We have to get to a place of trusting your divine intent, right?

Divine: The spiritual task is to continue. The benefit of presence—once you see what you see—is that you *know* what is coming. And, yes, maybe you fell blindly initially. The key in spiritual work is to walk into it by choice. I want you to learn the distinction between free will and compulsion. Suffering may have placed you on the path, but, eventually, you continue on the path voluntarily. Most people use their shadow and related fears as a force of motivation to continue. Watch your reactions but don't identify with them. Make a distinction between past and present fear. The question in spiritual work is always the same: To whom are you going to listen? The fearfulness and immaturity of a child lost? Or the wisdom and depth of an adult found?

Seeker: Do you, the divine, cause accidents or events to happen if we continue to ignore you?

Divine: Yes, I bring to you what you need to understand so you can let it go. Sometimes these events and lessons are not pain free. In fact, the pain can be the warning that makes you want to stop a particular pattern of behavior or thought. It is not a direct cause and effect relationship, but you do have a strong sense of my intents.

Seeker: It is difficult at times to see the light at the end of the tunnel in this work. How do you comfort us during difficult times?

Divine: Many people give different versions of how they come to know my comfort and presence. For example, you could be in a cold place, and your view could be blocked by the conditions of the moment. I may advise that you place your back toward what is blinding you. This will allow temporary warmth. I also warn to be careful though, as walking backwards can become a habit.

Seeker: It seems you are competent in preparing us to do spiritual work. Is this by design?

Divine: Yes, metaphorically I make you aware when you are walking with your back to the cold. It may feel warmer, but I also warn that you are moving blindly. On the other hand, if you turn into the cold, you will find shelter and a glimpse of a light at the end of the tunnel.

Seeker: Do we continue to move forward when that happens?

Divine: People try to stay forward, but eventually the ego and cold can turn them around again. Sickened and tearful from the ego's influence, they alternate between various choices, and this allows them time for reflection. Light or awareness is an occasional break in the weather. This is the nature of many people's lives.

Epilogue

Absence is the state of being away or apart. Such a condition exists in our culture because we tend to live in our thoughts. This means we use the body's energy to fuel our thinking and to ambulate from one place to another. Are we empty vehicles of absence? Is life lacking, or are we just away? Clearly on "automatic," we are experiencing this lack or absence internally as personal deficiency. Many of us are asking, praying, wishing, and even begging for our lives to be different: *Please ... whatever is missing ... can it please show up!?* This reinforces further that we are actually without something. Such a perspective is fast becoming a primary source of dis-ease in our daily lives. Who or what is absent? How do we get it back? Is it gone? Modern research and spiritual teachers suggest that *you* are away. Not *I* or *me* but *you*! Not your (i)dentity or personal (me)anderings—but the real You! Fact: Many of us are wandering aimlessly through life and without direction. A glimpse at the evening news or at the art of our culture reveals this astounding truth. It seems many of us are away!

If we are wandering without direction, what is our guide? I propose that we are missing the soul's intent. The soul's intent is our guide. As an above observer, the soul is not missing—it is just out of our awareness. When life has meaning and purpose, we are aware. When it does not, the soul's guidance is unconscious. As a result, we feel lost. The sages of modern times all agree: we are drowning in the thoughts of who we *think* we are. The soul has been relegated to the unconscious and invisible world of the internal. We experience the soul's intent as presence. Self-assured and confident of its place in our lives, we grow and grow others. Absent, we frustrate and anger ourselves. Whether this anger is directed inwardly or outwardly, everyone suffers from it. The soul's intent is that we arrive, get here, and be present, without punishing or blaming others for not being here. Presence allows an observation of our lives without judgment. It is the dimensional quality of love.

Like *Conversations with God* by Neale Donald Walsch, which showed people the world is in trouble and is confronted by events and conditions that warrant attention, *The Soul's Intent* brings the dialogue and reality closer to home. Before we become a planet that may or may not implode from spiritual confusion, we are human beings self-destructing, each alongside the other. This self-destruction is affecting everyone that we associate with. Saving ourselves from self-destruction is saving the world.

The Soul's Intent is a conversation with the soul—our own divinity. The questions posed are by seekers of its wisdom, all of whom are suffering with personalities that prevented them from feeling peace or contentment. Combined with an ethic of compassion for the self, they find a key to their journey—presence—and they are amazed by the clarity and continuity of the soul's answers. I have humbly arranged the conversation into a sequence that portrays a path of spiritual revelation and rebirth. *The Soul's Intent* is a wonderful example that a higher organizing intelligence is at work in our lives.

In *God: A Biography*, Jack Miles notes that philosophy has long seen god or soul as a projection of the human personality. If this is so, it is time to realize that humans are no longer projecting their personalities towards the heavens. Rather, they are planting these inner false images of themselves on their families, neighbors, friends, and—worse—their enemies. *The Soul's Intent* reveals the nature of introjection—taking into oneself—and the damage it can do to the human spirit. Unfolding as a process of self-discovery and arrival, *The Soul's Intent* wishes for us to get here—now. In doing so, we can then see where we are going. Locked into the images of the past, we are fearfully looking over our shoulders and blind to what is in front of us.

I have had years of experience as a counseling psychologist. Working with hundreds of poat-trauma patients and spiritual seekers, I have learned that there is much more to the human condition than polishing and managing our personalities.

The Soul's Intent identifies four stages of spiritual development. Where are you?

- The hesitant stage: Those who wish to be more self-expressive and have a better grasp of life. They have a vision of transformation, but are not prepared for how quickly this image can disappear. When the image does disappear, their lives and circumstances seem worse than before. Their pattern is to hesitate before they continue. During this stage, people struggle with depression and spiritual confusion.

- The balancing stage: Those who experience their duality or opposites. They become aware of their defenses, insecurities, social barriers, and boundaries of fear. Because they examine their inner images thoroughly, there is an understanding of how to gain emotional nourishment. These individuals have an epiphany the instant they get a glimpse of what they are seeking. Their gratitude evokes a balance and a strong need to experience the balance again. Theirs is a tearful and frustrating stage because they don't know what to do to bring back into view what they saw.

- The envisioned stage: Those who see a vision of the eternal. Theirs is a painful realization because, once they have such an image, it will not fade. Once it is in their awareness, this image of the eternal glows brighter and brighter. Past hopes and dreams help them remember the older traditional path. Not always aware of what is happening within them, these individuals just know to continue.

- The present stage: Those whose connections with the eternal are real and current. More evolved than the general population, they are vigorously creating as much energy as possible to benefit and transform others. Their wish is to "stay with" what they have discovered, and make it as available to others as possible. These individuals somehow know that they can "become" whatever they wish to become.

It is the aim of this book to show you that, though your spiritual journey may seem difficult, confusing, or without end, emotional satisfaction and transformation are possible once you know the soul's intent. Figure out what stage you are in, and please continue!

Glossary

Above Observer—A quality of the soul that fosters self-awareness. An aspect of the self that is figuratively higher than or superior to the ego that observes our lives without judgment or analysis.

Aya—Adinkra symbol for *fern* on front cover. Means endurance, independence, defiance in the face of difficulties; hardiness, perseverance and resourcefulness.

Divine—The ocean in which the soul is a tiny drop. Emanates from God. Being or having the nature of a god. To perceive intuitively or through an inexplicable perceptive power. Being of such excellence as to suggest inspiration by god. A broader meaning than deity as it refers to all that is of God including those aspects that have neither gender nor name.

Dreams—C.G. Jung: "The dream is a little hidden door in the innermost and most secret recesses of the psyche, opening into that cosmic night which was psyche long before there was ego-consciousness, and which will remain psyche no matter how far our ego-consciousness may extend."

Ego—The ego *seeks* a balance between primitive drives, morals, and reality while satisfying basic needs created by caretakers and culture. Its main concern is with the individual's safety, and it allows some drives to be expressed, but only when consequences of these actions are marginal. The illusions it can create to survive and justify its choices are infinite.

Ego (seeker) interviewing the soul (divine)—The *ego* is defined as an aspect of the self that seeks balance in its known reality. Unable to see its own reflection, it can only become self-aware when communicating with its above observer or divine essence—the *soul*. Figuratively higher than or superior to the ego, the soul observes our lives without judgment or analysis. The ego's inability to recognize itself or to see what it is doing makes it a *seeker*. Sensitive to the memories and emotions of its experiences, the ego questions everything a person thinks, feels, or does. Because the *divine* or soul encompasses all that can be intuitively perceived, it organizes our dream symbols into a series of answers. The context these symbols provide allows for a deeper understanding of our lives. Thus, it is the soul that provides us support when the ego doubts its choices. Without a connection to this larger perspective, many of us stay trapped in the past. The personality tends to seek a higher source when it is suffering. The soul's intent is that we understand our journey when things are going well.

(E)motion—Energy + motion. (E)motion represents energy in motion. There is a distinction between emotions and feelings. Emotions are tied to memories of the past and a re-enactment of a previous experience. Emotions are perceived by the brain. An individual thought would go nowhere without a charge from an e-motion. In contrast, feelings are reactions to the immediate moment and a state of presence. Feelings are perceived by the human heart.

Self—Is first incarnated and then assimilated through the living efforts of the individual. C.G. Jung: "The self, like the unconscious, is an *a priori* existent out of which the ego evolves. It is, so to speak, an unconscious prefiguration of the ego."

Shadow—According to C.G. Jung, the shadow is a part of the unconscious mind that consists of repressed weaknesses, shortcomings, and instincts. Jung wrote: "Everyone carries a shadow and the less it is embodied in the individual's conscious life, the blacker and denser it is." The shadow is instinctive and irrational, but not necessarily evil even when it might appear to be so. It can be both ruthless in conflict and empathetic in friendship. As a consequence, the shadow is prone to project; for example, turning a personal inferiority into a perceived moral deficiency in someone else. If these projections go unrecognized, they insulate and cripple the individual by forming an ever thicker fog of illusion between the ego and the real world.

Soul—According to many religious and philosophical traditions, the soul is a self-aware ethereal substance unique to a particular living being. It is thought to incorporate the inner essence of the living being, and to be the true basis for sentience. Soul is used in two senses: it indicates the ego and the spirit-body. The soul is animated by the spirit, while the physical body is animated by the soul. A person's thoughts, feelings, actions, behaviors, and comparisons are apprehended or developed out of spirit. It is both conscious and subconscious. C.G. Jung: "… the soul … must contain in itself the faculty of relation to God, i.e. a correspondence; otherwise a connection could never come about. This correspondence is, in psychological terms, the archetype of the God-image."

Spiritual—Acting within a shared experience of the world, where *spiritual* is best understood as a sense of meaning and purpose that is greater than the self. People are considered spiritual when they seek to grow from their personal suffering.

Unconscious—C.G. Jung: "This consists of everything we do not know, which, therefore is not related to the ego as the centre of the field of consciousness. The unknown falls into two groups of objects: those which are outside and can be experienced by the senses, and those which are inside and are experienced immediately. The first group comprises the unknown in the outer world; the second the unknown in the inner-world. We call this latter territory the unconscious."

Bibliography

Bly, Robert. *A Little Book on the Human Shadow.* San Francisco: Harper One, 1988.

Johnson, Robert A. *Owning Your Own Shadow: Understanding the Dark Side of the Psyche,* San Francisco: Harper One, 1993.

Jung, C. G. Edited by Violet S. de Laszlo. Translated by R. F.C. Hull. *Psyche and Symbol.* New Jersey: Princeton University Press, 1991.

Jung, C.G. Edited by Aniela Jaffe. Translated by Clara Winston and Richard Winston. *Memories, Dreams, Reflections.* New York: Vintage Books, 1989

Miles, Jack. *God: A Biography.* New York: Vintage Books, 1996.

von Franz, Marie-Louise. *Projection and Recollection in Jungian Psychology: Reflections of the Soul.* Translation by William H. Kennedy. Chicago: Open Court Publishing Company, 1980.

von Franz, Marie-Louise. *Shadow and Evil in Fairy Tales.* Boston: Shambhala Publications, 1995.

Walsch, Neale Donald. *Conversations with God: An Uncommon Dialogue.* New York: G.P.Putnam's Sons, 1996.

Willis, Bruce W., *The Adinkra Dictionary: A Visual Primer on the Language of Adinkra.* Pyramid Complex, 1998.

Zweig, Connie, and Jeremiah Abrams. *Meeting the Shadow: The Hidden Power of the Dark Side of Human Nature.* Los Angeles: Jeremy P.Tarcher, 1991.

978-0-595-50012-3
0-595-50012-9